POLICY AND PRACTICE IN EDUCATION

NUMBER FOURTEEN

ASSESSMENT

POLICY AND PRACTICE IN EDUCATION

POLICY AND PRACTICE IN EDUCATION

EDITORS

JIM O'BRIEN *AND* CHRISTINE FORDE

ASSESSMENT

Mary Simpson
Chair in Classoom Learning
The Moray House School of Education
University of Edinburgh

DUNEDIN ACADEMIC PRESS

EDINBURGH

Published by
Dunedin Academic Press Ltd
Hudson House
8 Albany Street
Edinburgh EH1 3QB
Scotland

ISBN 1 903765 45 5
ISSN 1479-6910

© 2006 Dunedin Academic Press

The right of Mary Simpson to be identified as the author
of this work has been asserted by her in accordance with sections
77 & 78 of the Copyright, Designs and Patents Act 1988

British Library Cataloguing in Publication Data
A catalogue record for this book is available from the British Library

Typeset by Patty Rennie Production, Portsoy
Printed in Great Britain by Cromwell Press

CONTENTS

EDITORIAL INTRODUCTION

This series is concerned with policy and practice in education. The area of assessment illustrates clearly the relationships between policy and practice and between policy makers, stakeholders and practitioners. Assessment has been one of the most contested aspects of Scottish education where policy makers have sought to shape the day-to-day practice of teachers and the learning experiences of children. Mary Simpson gives us a critical account of the development of assessment systems in Scotland from the introduction of Standard Grade to current concerns about formative assessment.

The book provides a detailed analysis of the development of policies on assessment, it relates these to debates about purpose of education and to the growing body of knowledge about how children and young people learn. It provides a historical view outlining the development of Standard Grade, *Higher Still* and particularly the campaigns surrounding the introduction of National Testing. From this the author then turns her attention to two current concerns. First, the question of where Scotland stands in relation to other nations in terms of educational performance and, second, the question of how assessment can be developed from a blunt tool for forcing change in a particular political direction to become a means of informing and enriching the learning experiences of children and young people.

This wider conception of assessment is a substantial element in this book in which the author tackles issues related to international monitoring and to the current emphasis on formative assessment. It is in the former area of assessment that the trend towards globalisation in education is particularly acute and issues related to national comparisons of pupil attainment are often reduced to shock headlines. In this study we go beyond the headlines to consider the important issues underlying the systems for national monitoring. In the account of formative assessment we observe the bringing together of policy, research and practice and see also how ideas of diagnostic and formative assessment have developed in Scotland.

Mary Simpson is Professor of Classroom Learning at the University of Edinburgh. She was involved in the development of assessment in Standard Grade and in the 5–14 Development Programme. Her main research interest has been in the use of diagnostic or formative assessment to understand learning and thus to contribute to the effectiveness of teaching. Since the 1980s she has made a significant contribution to the understanding of and continuing engagement with formative assessment by many Scottish educationalists on which the *Assessment is for Learning* initiative now builds.

Dr Jim O'Brien
Vice Dean
Moray House School of Education
The University of Edinburgh

Dr Christine Forde
Head of Department
of Educational Studies
The University of Glasgow

ACKNOWLEDGEMENTS

This is not a book on how to do assessment, but on why assessment takes the forms it presently does in Scottish schools. I have tried to give a balanced view of the past, the present and the future: the past – wherein lies the origins of so many of our present confusions; the present – in which so much is currently changing that it is difficult to see the overall picture; and the future – in which we rest out our hopes for more effective policy and practice and less burdensome demands.

I have been very well supported in my work by colleagues who were more knowledgeable than I and who gave generously of their time to read and comment on drafts, and who did their best to put me right on my many errors: Carolyn Hutchinson, Lindsay Paterson, David Raffe, Lillian Munro, Christine DeLuca, Judith Gillespie, Donald Gray, Jackie Heaton, Jennifer Kerr and Marian Grimes.

My special thanks go to Louise Hayward and Ernie Spencer who not only read and commented on several chapters, but who over several decades have been central to the development of policies that have tried to make the assessment systems in schools supportive to learners and professionally rewarding for teachers.

The book is dedicated to my husband Tom for all his support over the years, and to the many teachers who will still be struggling to make sense of assessment in the future when I am well and truly out to grass!

Mary Simpson

CHAPTER 1

ASSESSMENT IN A CHANGING WORLD

Just as the selective era determined one form of assessment, the monitoring era another and the accountability era several, the priorities and structures of education in the next century will determine the next era. Just as the past models were layers on top of each other, we will have further overlays but with many of the same structures and imperatives operating underneath. (Whetton, 1997, p. 119)

Scotland is a small nation in which an honourable educational past, in memory defined by proud certainty, has been replaced by realms of uncertainty. We now exist in a global arena, in which our small nation strives to prosper through modernisation, while still retaining its cherished values and identity. Assessment in schools, its forms, purposes and consequences, plays a central role in the perceived status and identity of the Scottish educational system – a system in which Scots feel a strong national pride and through which they determinedly assert their distinctiveness from the ways of England (Paterson, 2000a).

We are at the beginning of ambitious new policy initiatives in curriculum, assessment and school organisation and management which aim to effect significant changes in every classroom by 2007 (Scottish Executive, 2004a; 2004b; 2004c; 2004d). But it is as much of a 'fresh start' as any learner's first day at secondary school. Carried into engagement with it comes our understanding, attitudes and commitments from historical educational events which created the present practices, determine our current thinking and which will shape our future actions. If we are to understand and learn from the past successes and failures, shed unhelpful baggage and undertake the new policy journey with confidence, optimism and a realistic expectancy of success, we need to understand the topography of the rocky terrain of theory, practice and policy which we have already created. This book attempts to offer a contribution to the development of this understanding in the field of assessment.

Several themes that are common to many countries interweave throughout this account of how the interactions of policy and practice have shaped assessment in Scottish schools in the past and will continue to do in the future. The first is the way in which the Scottish government frequently formulated policy to manage and promote socially desirable aims and goals, in addition to changes in pedagogy and practice, using assessment as the driving mechanism. The second is the way in which the form which assessment takes is determined by our changing paradigms of how learning occurs and consequently how it can best be supported and measured. The third theme is the tensions and compromises between politics, policy, long established mindsets, cultural processes and valued practices which ultimately determine the outcomes of initiatives to change assessment.

Changing conceptions of assessment

For most of the period of universal schooling assessment has been summative and has taken the form of formal testing, the procedures and purposes of which reflected both the prevailing understanding of human intellectual functioning and the needs of society. Individuals were understood to possess an inborn and stable general component of intelligence that largely predetermined the efficiency of learning across all subjects and contexts. Learning was construed as a solitary activity requiring focused application, and one that progressed by the incremental acquisition of sequential component units of information and skills. Consequently, students learned individually, through transmission pedagogy and practice routines, and their acquired abilities and knowledge were assessed in controlled and decontextualised conditions in relative isolation from each other and from their teacher. Because the norm-referenced test scores subsequently derived from the associated assessments were attributed with the power of prediction of the student's trajectory through the hierarchical demands of the educational system, they were used as a means of selecting those relative few considered likely to succeed in higher education and thence to serving the governance of the state and industry.

Over the past four decades the developmental and cognitive constructs around which the objective, psychometric assessment edifice was constructed have been gradually undermined (Shepard, 2000). Cognitive and constructivist theories construed learning as 'making sense of the world', as the construction of meaning in terms of what the learner already knew, and as the development of higher order schemata and reasoning skills. Assessment then had to reflect the learner's ability to employ these schemata on unfamiliar, extended tasks, and consideration of the knowledge structures that defined the domain became essential. Open-ended, 'constructed-response' items that assess higher order knowledge and thinking, but which could be scored with modest effort and acceptable levels of reliability began to be incorporated into assessment. The more recent views on learning, the socio-cultural theories, turn from the question 'what do they know?' to the more challenging issue of 'what does it mean to know in this context?' and have only just begun to show an influence on thinking about knowledge transfer and assessment (e.g. Delandshere, 2002).

However, the initiatives that have resulted in the current systems of assessment in Scottish schools have been driven as much, if not more, by social, political and economic considerations as by educational ones. For example, in the 1980s a period of high youth unemployment meant an increasing proportion of young people stayed on in schools beyond the statutory leaving age and a suitable curriculum and associated assessment had to be developed to cater for this new client group within schools. This prompted *The Action Plan* and National Certificates (SED, 1983). By the mid 1990s a changing global economy increasingly suggested that a highly educated and skilled workforce was needed for a small nation to thrive on the northern fringes of Europe, and the necessity of including a higher proportion of the young population in continuing and higher education was indicated, largely shaping the curriculum and assessment developments within *Higher Still* (Scottish Office, 1994).

Scotland is now anticipating a decline in the school-age population and an increasingly ageing workforce. Consequently the educational system is striving more than ever towards equity, inclusion and equality in provision, recognising that while individual children are different in their academic attainments, they must be seen as equally valuable – and their diverse range of talents must be catered for appropriately. Employers are urging schools to develop the general skills of young people as much as their specific knowledge, and to imbue the workforce of the future with flexibility, independence and a predilection for engagement in life-long learning in order to engage effectively in the economic, social and cultural contexts and demands of the future – whatever these may be.

Recent policy initiatives attempt to prepare the schools to be responsive to this new social agenda. *A Curriculum for Excellence* (Scottish Executive, 2004a) that will begin a new wave of change, particularly in secondary schools, appears to be built on the premise that in addition to a knowledgeable and creative population, social responsiveness and collaborative participation are also prerequisite for societal cohesion (and economic competitiveness). This presages a new set of aims for schools, implies a significant change in curriculum and pedagogy and will require an innovative approach to assessment. And though this lies in the future, as indicated by Whetton in the opening quotation, whatever develops will have many of the current structures and imperatives still operating underneath.

Current assessment in Scottish schools

In Scotland, pupils progress through the formal school system in roughly three phases, experiencing a sequence of assessments designed at different times, and based on different principles of organisation (see Appendix 1). But the validity of all three systems rests on the principle that effective assessment samples a well defined and largely subject-based curriculum – a clearly delineated body of knowledge and skills which pupils are taught and are expected to learn. All are directed ultimately towards contributing to the overall aim of providing a coherent and progressive experience of learning in school for all Scottish children, with levels of curricular demand appropriate to their range of secure knowledge and skills, and with formal recognition of their attainment at transition and exit points. In addition to this summative purpose, these assessments have, to different degrees, taken account of the potential for assessment to be used to support and inform learning and teaching, and have additionally been deployed as monitoring instruments to assess the effectiveness of schools and teachers. The well-embedded practices of these existing systems and the associated mindsets will form the foundations on which the new assessment framework is being constructed.

The 5–14 curriculum

In the seven years of primary and the first two years of secondary school (age 5–14) pupils experience the 5–14 curriculum (L&T Scotland, 2005). During this time they will potentially have encountered up to six National Tests at levels A to F in language and mathematics, and informal teacher assessment in the other three areas of the 5–14 curriculum. These tests are not standardised. The items lightly sample a domain, they can be applied to pupils as individuals or in groups at any time, and are not 'high stakes' for the pupils, who progress steadily through the system regardless of their level of attainment or performance on the tests. Produced against considerable opposition during the 1990s, the tests were originally designed to assist teachers confidently to confirm pupils' progress through applying common standards to teacher assessments in the primary years. Their later use for monitoring purposes increased dissatisfaction with them and as part of the reforms in assessment in 2004 they have recently been redesigned and renamed National Assessments (see Chapter 2).

The Standard Grade courses

The development of Standard Grade courses during the 1980s for pupils aged 14 to 16 years introduced certificated courses which were designed for pupils across the attainment range, providing curricula, external examinations and certification at three levels of difficulty – Foundation, General and Credit and which were based on a criterion- or domain-referenced rather than a norm-referenced rationale for assessment. The

Standard Grade curriculum comprises fixed courses of two years' duration and requires pupils to study mathematics, English, a science and a foreign language, in addition to another four courses selected from a range of fairly traditional academic school subjects. Generally speaking, the larger the school the more choices a pupil will have – subject choice being dictated by the availability of staff and the exigencies of very complex timetabling. Regulations which did not allow any acceleration through the system from 12 to 16 years have recently been relaxed (L&T Scotland, 2001), and since the 5–14 levels of attainment have been extended by one level (to level F) and since the introduction of the Intermediate level National Qualifications the future of Standard Grade has been questioned. A review of Standard Grade currently in progress will report in 2006–7 (see Chapter 3).

The New National Qualifications
The system of New National Qualifications (NNQ) was fully implemented in 1999 following the publication in 1994 of *Higher Still – Opportunity for All* (Scottish Office, 1994) in which the government set out a programme of reforms for secondary education post Standard Grade. It comprises a unified scheme for all academic and vocational qualifications within a structure of modules and courses (which consist of 4 modules) in a progressive set of levels: Access; Intermediate 1; Intermediate 2; Higher and Advanced Higher (L&T Scotland, 2004). Schools typically provide opportunities for pupils to take the modular courses in up to five subjects in Secondary 5 at Intermediate or Higher levels, and in Secondary 6, the final secondary year, to move to the level above that previously attained in Secondary 5. In addition to providing a progressive series of qualifications that gave opportunity for all students to study at appropriate levels, a key aim of the *Higher Still* programme was to give parity of esteem to vocational and academic courses (see Chapter 4).

National monitoring of attainment
Since the 1970s Scotland has regularly participated in the major international surveys in attainment: Trends in International Mathematics and Science Study (TIMSS); the Programme for International Student Assessment (PISA); and Progress in International Reading Literacy Study (PIRLS). In addition, the overall performance of pupils in the educational system has been monitored since 1983 by the Assessment of Achievement Programme (AAP). To date these surveys have comprised 'high stakes' assessment for the policy makers only, however, the monitoring function of the national survey will be extended to Authorities in 2005 by means of the Scottish Survey of Achievement (see Chapter 5).

The 2004 policy initiatives

> Scotland needs a coherent and effective system of assessment that is clearly focused on promoting progress and learning. A new system should build on existing good practice rather than impose radical change. (Scottish Executive, 2001c)

The diverse societal prompts for changes, and the timing, tensions, compromises and pragmatic decisions taken during the curriculum and assessment developments from 1980 to 2004 (see Appendix 2) resulted in three quite different systems from age 5 to 18 and it had become clear by the late 1990s that in the 5–14 years in particular, the systems were increasingly unco-ordinated, incoherent in terms of purposes and application, and frequently misunderstood. Assessments designed for distinctive summative, formative and monitoring purposes had become misapplied, leading to a range of adverse effects, particularly that of 'teaching to the test' in classrooms, and the monitoring of school performance using data which was unreliable for that purpose (see Chapter 2). A range of the perceived difficulties and negative attitudes towards assessment was identified in the HM Inspectorate (HMI) review of assessment commissioned in 1998 by Helen Liddle prior to devolution (Scottish Executive, 1999).

By December 2000 responses to an initial consultation on the different ways in which improvement might be achieved had been independently collated (Hayward *et al.*, 2000). Three main areas of contention were identified which respondents suggested would have to be resolved if the assessment tools and the judgements of the profession were to be strengthened. Firstly, the tensions between assessment to support learning and assessment for purposes of accountability would have to be resolved. Secondly, teachers needed staff development, particularly with respect to engagement in 'moderation' activities on children's work at different levels to make teachers' professional judgements more secure. Thirdly, rationalisation of the processes of recording and reporting progress was needed. There was also evidence that testing had become dominant because teachers were often less aware of the actual policy and national guidelines than they were aware of the context of 'performativity' within which they perceived the policy to have emerged. From the teachers' perspective, the only 'hard evidence' that counted with the Inspectorate was test results (Hayward and Hedge, 2005).

There was, not surprisingly, little consensus on how to deal with summative assessment in the 5–14 curriculum years: while around half the respondents to the consultation wanted the abandonment of all such tests, equally as many thought they should be made more objective, reliable and standardised in order to give teachers and schools secure information about their pupils' attainment. In contrast there was considerable support for assessment undertaken by teachers for the purpose of supporting learning, although whether all respondents held the same view on exactly what this meant was not clear. Thus, although there was support for change and clarification, there was little consensus on exactly what the changes should be, but general agreement that, whatever the changes were, they should build on existing practice rather than introduce radical changes.

Since the inauguration of the Scottish Parliament in 1999, its members and leaders dealing with the public policy sectors – health and education in particular – have been forging policies that are in key respects different from those of their English counterparts and in harmony with the Scottish system and national ethos. As a result of the make-up of this government, a strong Labour–Liberal Democratic coalition, there has been insignificant political opposition to the general thrust of educational policy on purely ideological grounds. Additionally, with a former teacher, Jack McConnell, serving as Education Minister, and later as First Minister, 'partnership' has not only been the working relationship aspired to between politicians developing policy, so too, 'partnership' has been the modus operandi sought in education between central government, the Local Authorities and the teacher unions (see Pickard and Dobie, 2003). In order to bring coherence to the assessment systems in place for pupils age 3–18, a series of specific initiatives were set in train, which started with further consultation and action on changes in assessment and reporting 3–14, and culminated in the policy documents on assessment in 2004 and 2005 (Scottish Executive, 2004b; SEED, 2005a).

Following the parliamentary debate of 20 September 2001 led by the Minister for Education, Jack McConnell and the Deputy Minister, Nicol Stephen, an Assessment Action Group comprising key stakeholders and chaired by the Deputy Minister was set up. This group agreed that the programme of development which they would set in train would have the following broad aims:

- to develop a unified system of recording and reporting in the form of the Personal Learning Plan (PLP);
- to bring together the current systems for assessment of attainment, including the National Tests, the Assessment of Achievement Programme and the 5–14 Annual Survey;
- to provide extensive staff development and support through a project-based approach.

The Assessment is for Learning (AifL) programme was established in 2002. It was led by Carolyn Hutchinson, Head of the Qualifications, Assessment and Curriculum Division of the Scottish Executive and was designed to take forward the three aims above in the light of the views expressed in the consultation. Ten linked projects were established to explore how to take the programme forward (L & T Scotland, 2003). One set of projects was planned to support the development of teachers' professional practice in assessment and reporting as part of teaching strategies to support pupils' learning (Formative Assessment; Personal Learning Plans and their Management; Reporting to Parents; and Full Inclusion of Pupils with Additional Support Needs). A second group focused on assessment evidence and quality assurance of assessment judgements – 'sharing the standard' – in order to develop confidence in the validity, reliability and comparability of teachers' assessment judgements across schools and Authorities (Gathering and Interpreting Evidence; Local Moderation; New National Assessments; and the AAP). Each of the 32 Local Authorities was invited to appoint an assessment co-ordinator to manage and support the programme activity locally. Professional development was incorporated into each of the projects with the mechanisms for extending inclusion from the original core schools, which had been grant aided in their developments, highlighted as a key concern especially for the Authority assessment co-ordinators (see L&T Scotland, 2003).

The system which has emerged

At the formation of their second coalition government the Scottish Labour Party and the Scottish Liberal Democrats issued a *Partnership Agreement* in which the key references to assessment could not have been more designed to please the teaching profession:

> We will provide more time for learning by simplifying and reducing assessment, ending the current National Tests for 5–14 year-olds. We will promote assessment methods that support learning and teaching. We will measure improvements in overall attainment through broad surveys rather than relying on National Tests (Scottish Labour and Liberal Parties, 2003, p. 27).

The question remained: how exactly was this to be achieved? Were all formal forms of assessment to be removed from the primary schools? How were the local and national standards to be monitored? What data was needed to evaluate the 'health' of the system and the success of any new initiatives? A set of options was issued in the form of a questionnaire to schools, Authorities and other stakeholders, and a series of regional seminars providing a forum for discussions focused on the options was run by the Scottish Executive Education Department (SEED) and Learning and Teaching Scotland (L&T Scotland) in late 2003. This second round of consultations on specific options solicited yet another typically low response rate from the profession, and similarly produced no clear consensus on many key issues (Maclennan, 2004).

It was decided that whatever system was put in place, it had to deliver the following:

- sound, accurate professional judgements on the part of teachers in schools;
- quality assurance of those judgements at local and national level –'shared standards';
- a robust approach to national monitoring of attainment without negative impact on classroom practice – the gathering of quantitative data as part of a monitoring system had to be fitted in as 'an enduring part of the system'.

The key challenges therefore were to remove from the classroom any damaging 'high stakes' tests or collection of teacher monitoring data, and to substitute quality assurance through more robust and secure teacher engagement in assessment and moderation processes. The Government's final response to the consultations took forward the key issues identified in the consultation responses and the evidence of progress emerging from the programme of projects (Scottish Executive, 2004b). The new framework for assessment is summarised below (SEED, 2005a):

A coherent national system of assessment

Formative

Formative assessment	Local authority collection and analysis of information to inform provision and improvement
Personal learning planning	
Involving learners, and parents and other adults, in the learning process	HMIE inspection feedback and subject/quality/improving reports
	Follow-through inspection activities
Internal	**External**
Teachers' judgements and reports, with local moderation and National Assessments as part of understanding and sharing standards	Scottish Survey of Achievement P3, P5, P7, S2 National Qualifications (SQA) International studies HMIE inspections and reports on authorities and schools

Summative

The central monitoring of achievement at national and local levels is to be achieved by the Scottish Survey of Achievement and international studies (see Chapter 5). The performance of individual secondary schools will be monitored primarily through the publication of their Scottish

Qualifications Authority (SQA) certification data on National Qualifications. While the press publish provocative 'league tables' it has not been the policy of the Scottish Executive or the Local Authorities to do so. The collation of such data is intended to be used primarily to give formative support to schools, especially those whose data are seen to be out of line with statistics from schools with similar demographic characteristics.

The replacement of the National Tests with National Assessments delivered electronically (see Chapter 2) is part of the programme of local monitoring of pupil and school performance. The associated programme of moderation events is intended to assist teachers to 'share the standard' and thus develop their skills in effective assessment practices. The Local Authority now has responsibility for the gathering of a range of quantitative and qualitative evidence on the performance of its schools for formative purposes, and to plan the remedial support action to be taken to assist schools to achieve the best they can for their pupils. The overall aim is to foster the use of a range of dependable data, the limitations of which are understood, as a framework for comparing one's own provision and performance in relation to others in similar – or different – circumstances, as a means for planning improvement.

Activity in the internal, formative assessment quadrant is in many respects the most innovative and enterprising. This has been a central focus of school activity within the AifL programme, in which teachers develop not only formative assessment to change their pedagogical approaches, but include pupils more centrally within this process. However, the AifL initiative to develop formative assessment in practice also represents a unique experiment in policy implementation (see Chapter 6).

CHAPTER 2

NATIONAL TESTING AND ASSESSMENT

We in Scotland are justly proud of our school system. (SED, 1987)

With these reassuring opening words the Conservative government laid the velvet gauntlet of their proposals for curriculum and assessment reform down before the tense and expectant members of the educational community. They heard only the clank of the steel fist within. The most acrimonious and damaging period in Scottish educational development was inaugurated. It would leave a legacy of flawed assessment, confusion, mistrust and misunderstanding from which the profession and the processes of development of effective systems of testing and assessment are still trying to recover.

The educational context

The 1987 paper *Curriculum and Assessment in Scotland: A Policy for the 1990s* identified perceived weaknesses in the school system for 5–14 year-olds. These comprised: the variation in the nature and quality of in curriculum planning and management; lack of definition of the curriculum; lack of mechanisms to ensure progress in learning through primary and the early years of secondary; the curricular discontinuity between these two sectors at Primary 7 / Secondary 2; inconsistency in approaches to assessment and poor communication with the parents. The simplest and purest representation of the *educational* policy at the centre of the conflict was that teachers should engage in teaching activities which offered progression, continuity and coherence across the pupils' experience of primary and early secondary school, and that there should be some means of secure assessment of what pupils were learning as a consequence of these activities. There should then be a subsequent adjustment of the former in the light of the latter and parents should be offered clear accounts of their child's progress in terms of their actual attainment.

Every aspect of the developments which were set in place to take this apparently innocuous vision forward was contested and challenged.

While the academic, philosophical, ideological and professional debates on the proposed curriculum were pursued (Kirk and Glaister, 1994), the main public spotlight came to be trained on the decisions concerning assessment. What exactly was to be tested? Who was to set, apply and mark the tests? When were pupils to be tested? What were the results to be used for? There was a realisation that these were not simple operational questions, teachers felt they were about to lose significant control and autonomy and have imposed on them a system through which test results could be used politically and socially to call them to account, indicate value for money in education, and provide a lever for driving up standards.

The key protagonists

> Moreover, there was an understanding that testing was about more than education. It was about introducing the market ideology into education. It was also about undermining local government's power base. However, although this political dimension was widely understood, the key protagonists on both sides also understood that the campaign had to be waged only in educational terms, as the parents – who were the key audience – frequently complained that they wanted politics kept out of education. So, whilst the battle was highly political, sometimes bitter and personal, all the arguments were educational. (Gillespie, 1997, p. 1)

In the years between 1987 and 1994 as the superficially reasonable educational reforms were forged into agreed practice, National Testing, and its perceived begetter, the Conservative Minister Michael Forsyth, stood at the centre of the arena in which bitter confrontations between diverse political and social groups were played out. As Humes and Bryce (2000, p. 17) indicate: 'Ideology, bureaucratic systems and the networking of powerful individuals and groups have often been more potent influences in shaping policy outcomes than research evidence.' This was particularly true during the development of the 5–14 curriculum and the associated National Tests. In addition to central government and HMI, the main protagonists – each with their own competing and conflicting aims and agenda – included: the main teaching unions, particularly the Educational Institute of Scotland (EIS); the Local Authority education staff and local government committees; a variety of parents' organisations; the opposition MPs; the Consultative Committee on the Curriculum (CCC); the academic staff of universities and teacher education colleges; and last but not least – fuelling the flames of every debate with attention-grabbing headlines and stirring sound bites – the media. The widest ever, and most acrimonious, public debate on assessment was under way.

The political context

Scottish educationalists had a clear model against which to react. In England, over the years from Callaghan's Ruskin speech in 1976 to the passing of the Great Educational Reform Bill in 1988 there had been a wide-ranging education debate south of the border on such matters as defining the curriculum, standards of education of school leavers and how to monitor effectiveness of schools. As Daugherty (1995) indicates, there was not always a determined government agenda to take central control of education, but as the 'national' media daily reported English ministerial dictates and hostile teacher reactions it seemed to many north of the border that a right-wing 'Anglification' of the Scottish system through the specification of the curriculum and particularly through the introduction of 'National Tests' similar to the English Standard Assessment Tasks (SATs) was about to be imposed.

By the late 1980s there were few Conservative MPs in Scotland, and no Local Councils with Conservative majorities. At every level of public sector services, individuals, groups and organisations were increasingly disaffected and frustrated at being ruled by a Conservative government elected by English voters. While there was little consensus on what Scots were for in many areas, there was wide agreement on what they were against. As a follow up to the clashes over the poll tax, many welcomed another context in which national identity and rejection of Conservative ideology and values could be reasserted. The representation of all that many were against, politically and ideologically, came into focus in the person of Michael Forsyth, and the proposed reforms of the curriculum and assessment for the years 5–14. The teachers' unions had emerged successful from their confrontation with the government in the mid 1980s (see Pickard and Dobie, 2003) when their strike action over salaries and workload had brought considerable concessions in the Standard Grade development, and the main union was ready for round two with the Conservatives.

In Scotland, there been little serious challenge to the educational system. There had been no 'Great Debate' on education, no major public concerns about standards, and nothing like the William Tyndale School scandal to highlight the potential pitfalls of extreme and unchecked professional autonomy. Although many could cite some story of failure of the system for their child or children known to them, Scottish parents then, as now, were generally respectful of teachers' professionalism and authority. In some areas where there had been an influx of workers from beyond the UK or Scottish borders bringing parental groups that challenged the settled status quo and complacency of many public services, there had been no major engagement with the Scottish educational system. In Grampian Region for example, while determined, articulate and informed parents relocating from worldwide postings through the oil industry successfully harassed the Social Work Department for better services for their children with disabilities, alternatives to the state system were sought for the non-disabled siblings: the Dutch School, the American School and private education were the locations of choice. However, as Gillespie (1997) indicated, at the heart of the confrontations over National Tests was a battle to win over the hearts and minds of the parents. This had deep ideological provenance, was of key strategic importance to the main protagonists and contributed significantly to the form in which the tests emerged from the political fray.

The winning of the parental hearts and minds

In a paper produced by a group of right-wing Conservatives including Michael Forsyth, Peter Lilley and Michael Portillo, the authors identified their perception of the main defect in the UK educational systems: 'the complete domination by the producers' (Forsyth *et al.* 1986). They championed those parents in their constituencies who were disaffected: 'As parents they feel they ought to have a major say in the education of their children. They find themselves instead faced with a monolithic system which seems impervious to their preferences and insensitive to their criticisms ' (p. 5). Securing the support of parents in any confrontation with those in the educational system was therefore vital, and at first Forsyth secured the goodwill of the official parent consultation organisation, the Scottish Parent Teacher Council (SPTC). However, the power of a number of smaller proactive parents' groups, particularly the Lothian Parents' Action Group organised by Judith Gillespie and Education Alert organised by Diana Daley in Grampian Region, had already been successfully tested out during their opposition to the establishment of school boards and the possible introduction of other English-inspired reforms. Consequently, when the 1987 consultation paper was circulated, a pattern and leadership for organising parental opposition nationally had already been established.

When in 1990 the first detailed proposals for testing were published, in which tests at Primary 4 and Primary 7 were indicated, unconfirmed rumours of the possible reinstatement of an 11+ type test for segregating pupils and the possible prosecution of parents who withdrew their children from the testing raised the stakes and brought the Local Authorities more actively into the fray – as the bodies which had to monitor the withdrawals. With some enthusiasm, these opposition parties allied and set out to test whether Forsyth's professed commitment to parental freedom of choice extended to their freedom to withdraw their child from the tests. Some Authorities acted in ways that indirectly encouraged withdrawal; others 'allowed' it, '*schools positively encouraged it*' (Gillespie, 1997, p. 7; Munro and Kimber, 1999). From January 1991 a number of the smaller parental groups agreed to co-ordinate their activities under the banner of The Parents' Coalition lest their views and voices were dissipated in the cacophony of the political and professional debates. With Local

Authorities and the EIS thus allied so enthusiastically with the parents, Forsyth's aim of using the parents as consumers to curb the power of these unaccountable professionals appeared to have been well and truly thwarted.

The processes of educational development

While the proposals within the 1987 paper were educationally unremarkable, the underlying ideology, timing and political provenance represented a major challenge to the status quo of decision taking and development within the Scottish educational community. Much has been written of the 'consensus' model of curriculum development that operated prior to the 5–14 Development Programme (Boyd, 1994). In contrast, Humes (1986) identified a powerful 'Leadership Class', the members of which dominated the key decision taking processes of the educational systems. Regardless of the contrasting theories of how the national decisions were actually taken, and whatever the underlying ideology, translation into practice was left largely to individual teachers, and while it is certainly true that the Primary Memorandum of 1965 put the consciousness of a 'child centred' curriculum firmly into the minds and vocabulary of most teachers in primary schools (Darling, 2003), the translation of this widely accepted educational ideal into effective and imaginative practice had always been patchy. Teachers within their own classroom exercised almost complete autonomy, and it was not unusual for pupils to experience, for example, a completely disjointed mathematics curriculum as they moved from year to year between teachers independently choosing to use Fletcher maths, SPMG, or their Local Authority produced schemes. In other curricular areas, e.g. history, or language skills, lack of planning for progression in pupils' experiences and skills within schools was also evident. School reports were concerned with what had been covered, rather than what had been learned, accompanied by a vague placement of the child as at, above or below average, based on individual teacher's unmoderated and largely unarticulated standards. As Brown (1990) noted, 'comments about complacency are not entirely misplaced' (p. 69).

In the 1980s, in response to HMI concerns about the pupils' diverse and often sparse experiences in the idiosyncratic classroom activities which then comprised thematic work designated 'Environmental Studies' (SED, 1980), an expensive programme of profession-led curriculum development was inaugurated. Teachers who formulated possible models of assessment for the outcomes associated with the curriculum packs created by colleagues produced little coherent materials (PEDP, 1986; Powell, 1986). When a similar model of autonomous, profession-led development was proposed by the writers of the 10–14 Report (CCC, 1986), the government was perhaps understandably not impressed. They wanted a more attainment-focused delineation of the curriculum, and were determined to reconstruct and control the policy making bodies and procedures to undermine the autonomy and power hitherto exercised by the profession which they considered were not always applied in the interests of pupils, parents or the public (Humes, 1995). Nevertheless, they had to move carefully; there were not many Conservative MPs left in Scotland following the 1987 election, and Forsyth himself was sitting on a vulnerable majority in his own constituency. A route forward had to be found between the right-wing ideological 'quasi-market' model which had emerged in England (Hartley, 2003, p. 285) and been driven through by politicians against extreme professional resistance, and the development of a system which would both incorporate the key educational improvements which they sought for Scottish education and optimise the likelihood of getting these changes accepted and applied.

The system which emerged

In England, ten levels of attainment (covering age 5–16 years) had been specified, with subject curricula devised by external experts and with standardised tests in many subjects at several levels, also constructed by external subject experts. In contrast, the Scottish curriculum (age 5–14) was divided into five levels (Bryce, 2003) with tests in Mathematics and English proposed only at Primary 4 and 7. There was fierce initial opposition from the CCC and teachers who were inclined to a more holistic approach, based on theme work and exemplifying the child-centred philosophy of COPE (Darling, 2003). The guidelines for five sub areas of the curriculum were subsequently compiled by working groups convened as sub-groups of the CCC, and comprising school staff, teacher educators, Authority staff and HMI. Thus the profession, rather than outside academic subject specialists as in England, had the dominant role in devising the content of the curriculum guidelines and the construction of the tests, although some who could have contributed 'maintained an attitude of censorious detachment' (Munro and Kimber, 1999, p. 716).

Particular features of the curriculum they devised led to later intrinsic difficulties with the National Tests. The descriptors of expected levels of attainment were not based on empirical evidence on what pupils at different ages were then actually attaining since such information was simply not available in many areas of the curriculum – a prime purpose of the tests was to provide information on this. Nor were they devised by educators or researchers well versed in the developmental elements of complex skills, such as reading. The descriptors of progression in know ledge and skills emerged gradually as a mixture of diverse components which, in addition to the knowledge and skills selected by the developers from the then existing primary curriculum, included: skills which had never previously been specified (e.g. talking) in order to promote their inclusion in practice; activities, standards or aspects of teaching and learning aspired to, such as an investigative approach within Environmental Studies; even, it is rumoured, components which were clearly impossible to assess through tests, the inclusion of these being the ploy attributed to one development group to thwart the proposed National Testing. The descriptors were subsumed into a manageable number of attainment targets at five levels on the basis of what the profession considered most pupils at Primary 1–Primary 3; Primary 4; Primary 4–Primary 6; Primary 6–7 and Secondary 1–Secondary 2 (Levels A to E) would or should generally be able to do/understand. As Bryce (2003) notes, the final 5–14 documents offered very general curriculum guidelines – as indeed the development groups intended – they did not represent teaching and assessment blueprints, or specifications of clearly defined domains as required for robust test construction. In a formally constructed criterion-referenced system, the coherence of the domain to be tested would be a key prerequisite for an effective test. In the 5–14 guidelines, the attainment outcomes are a collection of disparate subject- related knowledge or skills or activities which it was hypothesised on the basis of professional judgement should be attainable by the majority – initially an unspecified percentage – at a certain age or stage in their schooling.

As indicated above, the thwarting of the perceived intentions of the Minister was high on the priorities of several key factions involved in the development, with the issue of accountability a main concern for many in the teaching profession. However, the domination of the 'wisdom of the profession' not only in the construction of the guidelines but also in the writing of items for the test, guaranteed that the tests, written for the purpose of confirming the attainment of some sub-set of the disparate set of learning objectives were technically very different from the formally constructed SATS of the system of National Tests in England which were daily discussed on the UK 'national' news bulletins. Nevertheless, in the EIS anti-test campaign they were represented as being similar, and as 'bringing back the qualie' (the 11+ test). The union spokesmen toured the teacher–parent meetings and other venues warning of the potential 'Anglification' of the Scottish system as a consequence of the proposed Primary 7 tests, which would give the Minister the tool needed for the segregation of pupils at age 11 thus undermining the Scottish comprehensive system. This campaign in defence of the idealised 'democratic and egalitarian tradition of Scottish education' (Humes, 1995, p. 123) won many hearts. The Labour-dominated Local Authorities largely opposed the proposed tests, but on diverse and contradictory grounds. In the presentation to the Parents' Coalition in Aberdeen in 1992 Fred Forrester, President of the EIS, argued against the tests as they would reinstate a fearsome 'qualie' type of examination which would blight the education of Scottish children; Douglas Paterson representing Grampian Regional Council denounced them on an exactly opposite argument – they were not constructed rigorously enough to have the power to be used effectively for any professionally precise monitoring of attainment – and he announced that Grampian Region planned to set up its own assessment unit for the purpose of devising and applying its own 'properly standardised' tests.

The Primary Assessment Unit had been set up within the Scottish Examination Board to co-ordinate the writing of the items by practitioners and the compilation of test catalogues from which teachers could select tests. However the EIS boycott advice to teachers not to open these packs (EIS, 1991) meant that many teachers were denied the information required to make an informed and objective judgement. Some who engaged with an open mind with their use and intended purpose gave a critical but balanced view of their flaws but also recognised their potential for further development as very useful professional tools for teachers (Mitchell, 1991). The Parents' Coalition set out clearly *'What Parents Want'* in their Newsletter and presentations: assessment of pupils' strengths and weaknesses; continuous assessment (to inform teachers); feedback – face to face with teachers and with improved report cards; reassurance about consistency between schools; reassurance on children's literacy and numeracy, as the core of learning; substantial resources to make it work. They did *not* want league tables to compare schools results, ranking of pupil performance on the tests, or the return of the 'qualie' and selection. The EIS declared complete solidarity with these laudable educational aspirations and the strength of the teacher–parent alliance was secure as with this united front they opposed the government plans for National Testing at Primary 4 and Primary 7. However, the final skilful strategic move in the confrontation was made by the new Education Minister in 1992–3 when with one final disconcerting decision he completely fractured the parent–teacher alliance and brought the tests into every classroom.

The fact that the tests were to be applied at Primary 4 and Primary 7 was the key feature which teachers and parents appeared to agree was the main difficulty. If thus applied the tests could potentially be used to monitor schools or teachers at those two stages and to sort pupils at entry to secondary school. The EIS opined that they were not against the tests themselves, but the way they were to be applied. In the Parents' Coalition survey of 1992, which had been funded by Local Authorities (mainly Strathclyde), parent respondents had rejected the tests as proposed at Primary 4 (71%) and Primary 7 (57%), but 85% were in favour of 'continuous assessment within national curricular guidelines' (Parents' Coalition, 1991). If the tests were to be truly formative and give information to teachers of the child's strength and weaknesses, they should, in logic, be used in a more continuous way. Confirmation of the level attained by the child should be done when, in the judgement of the teacher, the child was confidently ready to demonstrate key attainments within the level. The parents pursued this logic in their opposition literature; the teachers' leaders expressed solidarity – what professional could object to this sound educational argument? To the great surprise of many, the Conservative Minister of Education in 1992–3, Lord Douglas Hamilton, conceded. From 1993 he decreed that the tests could be used whenever teachers judged pupils to be ready. They would be applied as part of the ongoing activity of the class in line with the principle that they were merely to give confirmation of the teachers' judgement and give improved information to parents.

The parents were jubilant. The teachers were aghast. At a stroke, every primary teacher was now to be responsible for monitoring the progression of the children in their class through the application of the tests as appropriate, and from 1994 this would of course extend to include the teachers of Secondary 1 and Secondary 2 pupils. The fierce arguments set in train by the EIS against the tests had a momentum of their own. Against their executive's advice, the EIS members at the conference of June 1994 voiced their position: 'We do not want to decide when to test – we want to decide *not* to test' (*Scotsman*, 1994a), and they voted decisively for a complete boycott. The teachers were jubilant. The parents were aghast.

In an acrimonious exchange of letters in the press with the president of the EIS in July 1994 Diana Daly pointed out the EIS agreement with parents on support for assessments that would monitor progress and opposition to tests which might be used to mark children for life. Clearly, she argued, the National Tests were now examples of the former, not the latter. 'If partnership is to be other than a convenient semantic peg, trust in teachers' professional judgement must be more than simply an act of faith.' Judith Gillespie represented herself as 'a simple soul' who naively believed the teachers' rhetoric about commitment to assessment:

> When teachers and union officials up and down the country told me during the testing campaign that they liked the test material, that it could be used both to monitor the children's performance and to check that they themselves were working at the right level, that they would welcome the opportunity to use such excellent and free material, as long as they had control of when they used it and that it was properly integrated into the curriculum, I foolishly believed them. How stupid can you get? (*Scotsman*, 1994b)

Over the summer of 1994 it became clear from the newspaper headlines that the alliance between the parents and teachers was under severe strain. 'Parents' voices still loud and clear' (*Press and Journal*, August 1994); 'Chances of national tests boycott look to be fading' (*Courier*, September 1994). The Council of the EIS, following consultation with their regional executives quietly set aside their polemical political arguments against the tests and their threat of boycott and continued their opposition alone, primarily on the grounds of increased workload.

The practices and problems of National Testing

Any system of assessment and testing can only be as secure as the curriculum on which it is constructed, and on the match between the purpose underlying its construction and the actual use to which the results are put. Following the acrimonious, contentious and often inaccurate rhetoric of the development of the tests, professional understanding, use and management of National Testing emerged confused and suffered further from additional adverse influences related to both these features in the decade which followed. As indicated above, the curriculum guidelines were relatively incoherent as a blueprint for a formal assessment system, but rather than the tests being developed further in order better to serve the original purpose of giving confirmation of teachers' judgements, they were subsequently deployed for additional summative and monitoring purposes for which they were entirely unsuited. As Munro (2003, p. 746) indicates, 'they have both a summative and a diagnostic value within certain specified limitations'. These limitations have been regularly breached by teachers and headteachers seeking secure summative information and by local and central government for monitoring purposes.

The shaky curriculum foundations

The National Tests had represented a first attempt at an innovative approach to a more systematic assessment of valued complex learning in context – the classroom – and on the basis of general descriptors which teachers could readily recognise from practice rather than the type of theoretically based constructs from which the typical, narrowly focused, often behaviouristic criteria of criterion referencing are necessarily derived. National Tests based on such practice-based educational constructs can indeed serve the very useful professional functions aspired to by many at the inception of the tests: providing confirmation of teachers' judgement using common standards; assisting teachers to identify appropriate work for individual pupils; offering good quality information to parents and reassuring them of their child's progression; and promoting a degree of continuity in learning experiences at transition points between classes and schools. However, tests based on such loosely defined criteria, described by Sainsbury and Sizmur (1998) as 'abstract and complex notions of valued educational outcomes', cannot provide the kind of reliable summative information afforded by more narrowly focused, formally constructed and standardised tests such as the Edinburgh Reading Test.

Many clearly did not remember the unsatisfactory state of classroom assessment prior to 5–14 (recalled recently by Toner, 2004) and complaints began to be raised by teachers that the tests 'merely' confirmed their judgements, or did not give an 'accurate' assessment of a child's pattern of attainment in language and mathematics. The tests were clearly not designed to do the latter, but they were subject to this criticism particularly by the secondary teachers who looked for test results accurate enough to support setting and who, generally maintaining their global antipathy from the heady days of their boycott campaign, simply failed to apply them. By 1997 only about 10% of secondary school English and mathematics departments were applying the tests. Perhaps more seriously, the majority were also failing to use any records from the primary schools: 'in terms of continuity and progression for the individual pupil, the entrenched preference for a "fresh start" and lack of interest in records and work sent by pupils' previous teachers remain a cause for some concern' (Harlen, 1996, p. 31). The information communicated with respect to the test outcomes was either not understood, not trusted, or not acted upon (Simpson and Goulder, 1998a). Typically in secondary classrooms, little group work is done, certainly few teachers manage groups of pupils at different levels of attainment in the way that primary teachers do – a strategy for differentiation that makes the management of 'testing when ready' a little easier. As far as many secondary classrooms are concerned, most teaching and learning involves the whole class, and is lock step; all tests are sat at the same time; tests are for passing or failing; and outcomes are used to set pupils according to ability. Even in 2000, some school managers reported that the spirit of 5–14 had 'barely penetrated' many secondary classrooms (Boyd and Simpson, 2000; 2003), and Wilson (2003) indicates that 'only around two thirds of mathematics departments have fully implemented 5–14'. From the mid 1990s the inspectorate began through their reports to put pressure on the secondary schools to implement all aspects of the 5–14 curriculum and assessment, particularly in the light of the consistently disappointing performance of Secondary 2 pupils as judged from their inspections, and in the AAP surveys (see Chapter 5). In the late 1990s the Authorities were given a mechanism for requiring secondary schools to take account of National Tests. Unfortunately, this new requirement ran completely counter to the original purpose and nature of the tests.

Bearing the burden of target setting

Despite their earlier avowed antipathy to the tests (Worthington, 1990), the incoming Labour government retained them in their final more friendly form, but set the clock back by significantly raising the stakes of their summative and monitoring role. First published in 1996, 'How Good is Our School?' (HMIE, 2002) had set out to give schools quality performance indicators for planning and managing self-evaluation. These performance indicators were qualitative in nature, and were increasingly used by schools to examine and improve many of their processes and procedures. However, the operating principle in schools appeared to be that if the inputs were adequate, the outputs would take care of themselves. Data from the international surveys and the AAP seemed to indicate this might not be the case. There certainly appeared to be room for improvement in the attainment levels in Secondary 1 and Secondary 2. So increasingly the Scottish Office Education and Industry Department (SOEID) expected that quantitative data would be collected, collated and scrutinised as indicators of a school's effectiveness in securing appropriate attainment levels. In 1998 the report of a Ministerial Action Group on Standards in Scottish Schools, *Setting Targets – Raising Standards in Schools* set out frameworks of targets as an aid or spur to improving pupils' attainment levels. Just as teachers were required to set targets for their individual pupils (next steps), schools were to set targets for their own performance. But national targets for the percentage of pupils expected to attain at different levels of the 5–14 tests had also been set (Scottish Executive, 2002a), with the requirement that individual schools in which test results fell short would have to negotiate stepwise improvement year on year until the national targets were met or exceeded. Thus National Test results that originally had been intended solely for the use of teachers and parents were now required to be reported to the Authorities who in turn reported them to central government in the form of the Annual 5–14 Survey (Scottish Executive, 2004e). They consequently became high stakes tests – not for pupils, as their progression through the school or life chances did not depend on their performance – but for teachers, headteachers and Authorities. The tests were now being used quite inappropriately for school monitoring purposes.

For tests to have the level of reliability and validity needed to produce data robust enough to support such formal national auditing purposes requires extensive specialist statistical procedures (e.g. see Whetton *et al.*, 2000; Massey *et al.*, 2003). The Scottish National Tests simply could not provide such robust data. The assessment tasks were set in different contexts, and provided for a variety of response modes in order to minimise the negative effects typically associated with more formal assessment. Teachers could select the tests their pupils were to sit, and overt or unintentional teaching to the test almost certainly occurred. The reported attainment levels fluctuated about an upward trend, but alongside other data – from school inspections, the AAP, international surveys and the use of standardised tests by some Authorities – the measures afforded by the National Tests appeared somewhat unreliable. Given their content, structure, the processes of selection, application, marking and lack of moderation, it was hardly surprising that National Tests finally lost all credibility as a consequence of the mismatch between use and design through the demanding range of formative and inappropriate summative and monitoring uses to which they were now being put.

Revised tests for the future

> We will provide more time for learning by simplifying and reducing assessment, ending the current system of National Tests for 5–14 year-olds. (Scottish Labour and Liberal Parties, 2003, p. 27)

By the end of the 1990s, the concerns about National Testing had drifted to the periphery of the main political arena and the debate had for the most part become more honestly educational. Some within the practice of education and particularly within the teachers' trade unions still argued for the abolition of testing, but by 1999 the heart of the argument was centred on how to improve the perceived flaws in the existing assessment and testing systems. 'A previously implacable opponent of testing, Fred Forrester of the EIS, acknowledged that he had been wrong to fight against testing and that it was proper to have objective and reliable means of measuring pupil attainment in 5–14' (Munro, 2003, p. 752). While the intensely negative political associations had largely dissipated, the emotional and professional antipathy to the National Tests, and the subsequent professional confusion over their legitimate use and limitations remained. Their potential to be honed to become more useful as classroom assessments for teachers was by then completely obscured by their ineffective use as high stakes monitoring instruments and summative measures of pupils' attainment.

In order to identify the exact nature and perceptions of the anomalies, dissatisfactions and difficulties which were now inherent in the assessment and testing systems associated with ages 3–14, and to suggest possible action for improvement, the Minister for Education in 1998, Helen Liddell, asked for a review by HMI. This was published in December 1999, and summary accounts were widely distributed, soliciting responses to questions on specific issues and on possible ways forward (Scottish Executive, 1999).

Responses were received from 108 individual teachers, 59 schools and 78 other organisations (e.g. Authorities, School Boards, Professional Associations) (Hayward *et al.*, 2000; Munro, 2003). That changes should to be made to the National Tests was supported by 48% of respondents. The grounds given suggested a wish for the tests to be refined as summative instruments, e.g. that the tests needed to be made more reliable and valid, and needed to be used more consistently in the interests of standardisation. Those who did not support any changes (41%) felt that the current system which was not designed for monitoring could be made more effective for classroom use; that changes rested on a workload issue, and that extensive staff development would be needed to make any changes effective.

Some 50% of respondents did not favour the introduction of externally set and marked tests, primarily on the grounds that this would be likely to increase anxiety amongst children, promote coaching, and introduce biased importance into tested areas of the curriculum. The 44% who supported such an introduction did so on the grounds that they would provide a more accurate picture of the attainment at key transition times; they would afford comparisons to be made between pupils and schools; help establish national standards; and lessen teachers' workloads. There was a complete 50 : 50 split by respondents on the introduction of tests applied at fixed times. Clearly there was no consensus on any major point and whatever was to be done would not please around half of the respondents. The degree of disengagement of the profession from decision taking to deal with the difficulties was evident in the appallingly low response rate.

A second consultation document was released in the autumn of 2003 in the form of a questionnaire, giving several specific options and asking for preferences to be indicated. The response rate was again appallingly low.

> The majority of respondents were of the view that the current provision of test materials should not end but at the same time most respondents were in favour of a New National Assessment Bank . . . However, the diverse views on the use to which the materials were to be put flagged up the inherent tension in trying to have an assessment system which serves both the support for learning purpose and the accountability purpose. (Maclennan, 2004, p. 9)

With respect to the specific options offered on the development of the AAP (see Chapter 5), up to a third of the respondents did not engage with the questions, many of these indicating that they were insufficiently informed about the existing system to make any comments.

In order to cut through the confusion, SEED appear to have recognised and responded to the need to completely separate the systems for formative and monitoring use (Scottish Executive, 2004b). The monitoring function is to be taken over in 2005 by an extended AAP and will, through the light sampling of pupils, give information applicable only at national and Authority level (see Chapter 5). The National Tests are now renamed National Assessments, but their key intended role remains confirmatory (see Chapter 1). They comprise collections of items used in previous AAP surveys, and a test at any specified level can now be downloaded from a dedicated website site (www.aifl-na.net) as required by the teacher, copied and used with those pupils she feels are ready to demonstrate competence at that level. It is planned that this assessment bank will be extended, e.g. to include core skills and science.

> Will assessments drawn from the AAP prove any more valid and reliable? AAP items, based on nationally representative samples of pupils, will have an assured pedigree in terms of item information and therefore should be able to be used with a high degree of confidence. However, tasks and individual items will still vary in difficulty threshold, and threshold scores will still have to be set. Whether teachers' perceptions of the usefulness and reliability of the tests will be different remains to be seen. (Munro 2003, p. 753)

CHAPTER 3

THE STANDARD GRADE DEVELOPMENT

Because they are more carefully explicated, criterion-referenced
tests typically provide us with a more fine-grained analysis of
exactly what the pupil can and can't do. The differential skills we
hope learners will acquire can be more accurately portrayed via
a well described criterion-referenced test in contrast to its more
amorphous norm-referenced counterpart. And for promoting
instructional improvement, accurate diagnosis is an indispen-
sable first step. (Popham, 1973)

The context of the development

The main aims of the introduction of Standard Grade in the early 1980s
were to increase the breadth of studies undertaken by students in
Secondary 3 and Secondary 4; to cater for students across the full range
of academic abilities; and to improve access to national certification for
all students, particularly those from disadvantaged social backgrounds. In
the 1970s the development and use of criterion-referenced tests were in
their infancy – even in America where they had largely originated – but
this new approach to assessment appeared to offer the Scottish system a
tool for changing not only key aspects of education, but to serve important social and economic goals.

Although the introduction of comprehensive schools in the 1960s had
reduced some degree of social inequality, within these schools pupils
were still differentiated through streaming into certificated and non-
certificated courses. The majority of pupils left school as soon as they
legally could at age 16 and without any recognised qualification. The
Munn and Dunning reports of 1977 set the scene for profound changes in
the secondary curriculum and assessment in the middle years of 14 to 16
(SED 1977a and b), continuing the long steady progress over many
decades of the extension of education at secondary level to an increasing
proportion of the population and the erosion of the division of students
into 'the select few and the damned majority' (Paterson 2000b, p. 26).

Over the 1980s the development and introduction of the new certificated criterion-referenced model of assessment was arguably the most ambitious of all centrally directed policy initiatives, attempting as it did to drive change on a number of educational and professional fronts.

The innovative aspirations of the policy makers

The main change in the curriculum enacted in the Standard Grade development was the establishment of two-year long courses at Foundation (F), General (G) and Credit (C) levels which allowed pupils aged 14 to 16 years who had not previously had access to certificated courses to engage in almost the full range of academic subjects but at levels judged to be appropriate for their stage of understanding at the end of Secondary 2. Some bodies (e.g. the Consultative Committee on the Curriculum) initially envisaged that the three levels were to be progressive, with those who had an F level award able to continue onto G and later C. This would have been a step towards a progressive experience, but was a move that the organisation and understandings within the secondary school system did not manage to accommodate at that time. Consequently the new mid-secondary two-year courses remained traditionally stratified and lock-step, although some pragmatic flexibility was admitted by allowing class levels to overlap, F/G and G/C, and the early practice of allowing pupils to 'hedge their bets' by sitting two grade level examinations has remained. Although the organisation of the curriculum was based on the Munn framework of 'modes of learning' derived from the philosophical analysis of distinctive ways of knowing by Hirst (1969), in practice they were delivered within the traditional school subjects and specialisations within the teaching profession which form a UK-wide, and indeed, an international constituency.

Changes in the teaching of aspects of subjects were driven through the introduction of assessed 'elements' such as practical skills, talking, and problem solving. The underlying intention was to undermine the domination in the curriculum of the transmission of relatively inert subject knowledge, and to promote more active learning in the classrooms. Conversely, for subjects such as Physical Education and Home Economics, whole areas of these curricula were theory linked for the first time and written assessment work was increased.

Two paradigm changes in thinking relating to ability and to instruction were also associated with these developments. As Brown in an influential and authoritative review (1980, p. 5) noted, some advocates of criterion referencing 'appear to have an optimistic view of learning where ideas of innate ability take a back seat, all pupils are expected to master the work (although not necessarily at the same pace) and assessment is seen as an integral part of *instruction*'. However, the ideas typically held on innate ability were not easily sloughed off and although Drever (1985) explored the theory and practice of mastery learning as a means to 'creating conditions conducive to pupils' learning', the default position of pupils' personal characteristics being seen as the main determinants of success in school learning rather than aspects of the teaching contexts, largely prevailed.

The second challenge to mainstream thinking and practice was the indication that assessment should be used to inform instruction, not used merely as a terminal judgement on the pupils' attainment. At its most basic level, criterion-referenced assessment certainly provided a clearer picture than before of what pupils had failed to learn. And if there was no automatic assumption that this was due to lack of intrinsic ability, diagnosis demanded that either the teaching was scrutinised, or the understanding of the pupil was probed to find where the difficulties lay. Several initiatives to develop this approach in classrooms were launched, and although the Grade Related Criteria were used in a weak formative sense to assist pupils to identify and focus on the required learning, the strong linking of the assessment procedures to external certification largely squeezed out further development of these ideas, with their re-emergence two decades later in the AifL programme (see Chapter 6).

The 'reality check'

The development as it unfolded clearly exemplified the tensions which inevitably arise between the potential for authenticity in assessment which is aligned with the complex and diverse contexts of curriculum and learning; the requirements of reliability in a national certification system; and manageability in terms of teachers' and pupils' time. The Scottish Examination Board and many secondary teachers were – and still are – concerned that the integrity of the national certification process should not be compromised and that an award in one subject should be recognised by society as having the same value as a similar award in another subject. The edifices of secondary, further and higher education currently rest, perhaps with illusory security, on this long established foundation. The initially proposed 50% contribution of internal assessment at all three levels (F, G and C) was impossible to maintain through the unco-ordinated, idiosyncratic curriculum and assessment developments of individual schools or pilot groups – however well founded in the innovatory expertise of teacher enthusiasts. The requirement to abandon promising lines of school-based development to conform to some later centrally imposed assessment procedure alienated many committed school staff who were involved in the early piloting (Eleftheriou, 1985; Simpson, 1986). The teaching unions, whose members felt increasingly overwhelmed by the growing scale and demands of the developments and nursing discontent over pay and conditions, initiated carefully orchestrated strikes and blanket boycotts of development work. The initiative was rescued by the implementation of the significant revisions suggested by the Standard Grade Assessment Review Group – the 'Simplification

Committee' as it was commonly called (SGROAG, 1986) convened to salvage the development from the mounting complexity of the assessment system being developed and the growing ill feeling from the profession. A similar process had to be implemented during the development of *Higher Still* in the form of the Liaison Group (see Chapter 4). In the assessment procedures that emerged, manageability and reliability prevailed, although the courses that were designed did provide the spark for significant changes in learning and teaching, supported by dissemination of good practice, which had been one of the key aims of the initiative.

The positive impact of the courses and assessment which emerged

Through projects such as *Foundation Item Banking Science* (FIBS) (Arnold *et al*., 1984) it had become clear that professional skills in linking specific objectives, however simple, to assessment items were not very secure, nor were the conceptualisations of distinctive assessable domains or 'elements' within different subject areas. However, the widespread involvement of teachers in the Joint Working Parties that developed each course and in the subsequent development of test items for examinations and internal assessments, significantly advanced the knowledge and expertise of the profession. Although both internal and external assessment contribute to the final grade of the certification, the internal assessment is minor in scale and concerned with specific aspects such as talking or practical work which cannot be readily assessed externally. Thus the difficulties associated with the relationship between these two which later caused significant problems in the New National Qualifications were avoided (see Chapter 4). Much has been learned in the examining bodies of managing the complexities of Grade Related Criteria in assessment for certification, using constructs which may have less statistical integrity but more pedagogical utility than the previous frameworks for national examinations. The use of assessment items reflecting the outcomes to be taught and assessed has improved out of all recognition, and the assessments are consequently fairer, and more linked to the curriculum actually experienced by the pupils. The range of methods of presenting the questions and the modes of responses are now much broader. Changes such as these, however, as Whetton (1997) has noted, can occur largely within the psychometric tradition. And although revolutions in teaching undoubtedly occurred, the paradigm shift towards teaching and assessment more aligned with modern learning theory and with authentic form of assessment (see Chapter 7) requires considerably more loosening of the strong links with externality, standardisation and narrow concepts of reliability (Bryce, 1993).

The positive impact on pupils: entitlement and equality

With respect to attainment, the introduction of Standard Grade led to a much bigger proportion of the cohort than previously gaining qualifications and in a wider range of subjects (Raffe, 2003). Undoubtedly too, it reduced the educational gap between those pupils who came from socio-economically advantaged backgrounds and those who did not. All pupils are now required to study mathematics, English, a science and a foreign language, in addition to up to another four courses selected from a range of fairly traditional academic school subjects. Thus all pupils gained access to certificated academic courses, and the data from assessment indicates that the previously low attainment of disadvantaged pupils has been raised by the greatest amount. However, a significant gap still remains: students from advantaged social backgrounds have maintained their places at the top levels of examination scores. And as judged by the international survey data, unlike those of some countries, Scotland's statistics still show a concerningly long tail of low attainment (see Chapter 5).

Another achievement relates to the reduction in some gender inequalities, particularly the disadvantages in the past perceived to be experienced by females. The requirements and the choices in subjects, in theory, remove the possibility that schools might make different curriculum provision for boys and girls. In practice, however, the reality of classroom experiences may differ as a consequence of a range of factors such as peer pressures or perceived gender role differences exemplified in the teachers. Consequently the patterns of choices still show gender influences which are more pronounced among working-class pupils than among middle-class pupils (Croxford, 1997; De Luca, 2003). Nevertheless, an analysis of examination data by Croxford *et al.* (2003) identified gender differences in overall attainment levels which showed that patterns of higher levels for females over males are not a recent phenomenon, and not confined to secondary assessment outcomes. At Standard Grade, females gain more Standard Grade awards than males on average, and the largest differences in performance are found at the highest level of awards.

The future of Standard Grade

The development of Standard Grade absorbed so much time and energy within the system that for some time views that some courses were flawed, dated or out of step with much emerging educational thinking on learning and assessment and with other policy initiatives could scarcely be voiced. However, as the 5–14 programme was established, describing progressive stages in learning ('this child is at stage or Level B' – rather than 'this is a B level child'), and when the *Higher Still* programme streamlined the 16 to 18 curriculum (see Chapter 4), the two-year long, fixed syllabus courses of the middle secondary years began to come under pressure. The disjunctions between the curriculum organisation and descriptors of the 5–14 curriculum extending to level F on one side, and the staged progression of Intermediate 1 and 2 on the other (see Appendix

1) has led many to the conclusion that the anomaly of Standard Grade must now be formally dealt with. The curriculum review group established to take forward *A Curriculum for Excellence* (Scottish Executive, 2004d) will be examining the relationship between Standard Grade and the National Qualifications and will be reporting with recommendations in 2006–7.

Meanwhile, as the schools and Authorities have been given increasing freedom to be more flexible in the timing and procedures of their curriculum organisation, different solutions have emerged (L&T Scotland, 2001). For some, the slow pace of their pupils' experiences in Secondary 1 / Secondary 2 and the patchily implemented 5–14 curriculum are seen to be the problem, and these two years have been condensed into one, allowing Standard Grade to proceed as before, but starting in Secondary 2 (Payne *et al.*, 2004). Alternatively, in some schools, Standard Grade has been replaced by Intermediate 1 and 2 in selected subjects for example in the science (F/G) course, although in the view of the Inspectorate, while this has removed a course which was 'dated and inappropriate', the expedient of its replacement by the Intermediate courses 'has not been entirely successful in meeting the full range of pupils' needs' (HMIE, 2005, p. 17). Further, the decentralised ad hoc arrangements made within schools on a department by department basis is threatening 'to recreate precisely the kind of incoherent learning experiences formerly associated with combinations of SCE and SCOTVEC provision which *Higher Still* had been introduced to remove' (Howieson *et al.*, 2004, p. 186).

The Standard Grade development could be regarded as a successful use of a traditional concern for examination results to drive policy determined changes in teaching practices. In this it was successful and provided courses with curricula immensely richer than those that had previously existed. In retrospect, the initially proposed scale of assessment changes was simply too ambitious and wide-ranging for any system to accommodate. Only a few in Scotland had read about and understood the complex technicalities of criterion referencing (Brown, 1980; Bryce, 1993; Sizmur and Sainsbury, 1997), the details and implications of which are fairly impenetrable, except to the dedicated. The organisational and procedural structures of the secondary schools and the external examination systems were too rigid and the professional mindset of those working in and managing these spheres too traditional and risk aversive to allow of any truly innovative restructuring such as cross-curricular links. Whatever emerged from the potentially revolutionary policy visions had, in many respects, then as now, to be trimmed to be compatible with what already existed and what was considered practicable within the existing school practices and structures.

CHAPTER 4

THE NEW NATIONAL QUALIFICATIONS

> How has it come about that a programme whose principles are welcomed by all but those few thirled to a distorted, romantic picture of Scottish education circa 1900 is now so controversial in schools and colleges throughout Scotland? (MacBride, 1998, p. 6)

In Scotland there have been two major initiatives, *The Action Plan* and *Higher Still* that have sought to improve the range of and relationships between courses and their assessment in the post-compulsory years (Secondary 5 to Secondary 6). Along with comprehensivisation and the introduction of Standard Grade they continued a series of measures that contributed to the creation of a system of inclusive, universal, secondary and post-compulsory education and training in Scotland. Recent proposals for a unified framework for education for 14 to 19 year-olds in England were rejected, despite wide educational support, reportedly because of political timidity ahead of the 2005 General Election (DfES, 2005). However, in Scotland, a flexible and unified system has been introduced, with the single aim of 'meeting the needs of all categories of candidates'. Since 1999 it has attempted to meet this aim by catering for the full age and attainment range of pupils aged 14 to 18 years in both academic and vocational courses within the comprehensive school system and Further Education sector. In this chapter the origins and characteristics of this unified system are explored and the successes achieved and the difficulties still to be resolved are examined.

Why were the New National Qualifications introduced?

The history of policy making in the twentieth century regularly illustrates the conflicts between two ideals within the system: the 'open ideal' in which educational opportunity is kept open, locally available, and not inhibited by artificially high standards; and the 'closed ideal' which valued opportunity considerably less than securing, in the name of economy and standards, forms of schooling which involved selection and the identification of elites (McPherson, 1992a; 1992b). The series of policy enactments which included the comprehensivisation of the secondary schools, the raising of the school leaving age, and the replacement of O-grades by Standard Grade (see Appendix 2) had been key elements in the long history of the uneasy transformation of Scottish education from a relatively closed system, in which assessment was used to select and favour those few considered capable of achieving career enhancing awards on leaving school or university, to a more open one which aimed to include and serve the needs of the majority of Scotland's citizens, and in which assessment was used to recognise and reward achievement at many levels.

The Scottish comprehensive schools were judged by most independent evaluations to be successful. They were found to have raised attainment for all social class groups, but to have raised it most for working-class pupils. The Standard Grade reforms similarly evidenced a positive effect on social equity, with many more pupils securing qualifications that recognised their attainments at different levels, and reducing gender and social class differences by giving unbiased access to a broad curriculum. As in England, the curriculum of the secondary school remained organised around the academic disciplines, and indeed, this was considered to be one of the strengths of the comprehensive model, allowing everyone access to subjects that had previously been the purview of only the academic minority. When, in 1982, in the context of very high youth unemployment, the Thatcher government introduced the Technical and Vocational Education Initiative (TVEI) to make Further Education more relevant to the world of work, the Scottish educational establishment rapidly developed an alternative that reaffirmed the independence of policy and educational practices north of the border. The new qualifications introduced by *The Action Plan* (SED, 1983) comprised a suite of National Certificate modules administered by the Scottish Vocational Educational Council (SCOTVEC).

These qualifications were primarily aimed at reform of the curriculum, pedagogy and assessment in Further Education and it was expected that the take up in schools would be limited and largely confined to winter leavers and less academic students. However, they were used as a means of widening the curriculum (e.g. in personal and social areas and in technology), of offering progression where there was no Higher available in the school, and as a safety-net for those in Higher courses. Although perceived by teachers and by pupils as low status, the uptake was considerably more than originally anticipated (Croxford *et al.*, 1991). These qualifications had several key features which became of supreme importance in the subsequent developments. The first was their modular character: instead of courses lasting one or two years they comprised Units of a notional 40 hours' length. This structure allowed for regular updating in the face of rapid economic and technological change, and for flexibility in forms of delivery in different settings and to a more diverse group of learners – some of whom, for example, might not be in full time study. Secondly, they were designed to be taught towards the attainment of fairly specific and readily demonstrated skill-based learning outcomes regardless of the specific process and context of learning. Thirdly, these externally specified competences were internally assessed, with external moderation, giving a simple pass / fail judgement. Pupils could re-sit the assessment to convert a fail into a pass. Such a narrowly conceived notion of education in terms of these outcomes was disputed at the time even when applied within vocational education and training. However, greater controversy erupted when modularisation and the associated assessment principles were later applied to academic courses.

The 'Holy of Holies'

There have been several moves since 1945 to reform the structure of the Higher Grade examination, all concerned primarily with the suit-ability of the Higher as a preparation for higher education, and all abortive. (McPherson, 1992a, p. 114)

Sitting aloof from the changes which had periodically occurred in the examination systems in the secondary school during the twentieth century sat the academic 'Holy of Holies', the qualification which had been the jewel in crown of the Scottish educational system for more than one hundred years and had come to symbolise the continuity and distinctive-ness of Scottish education (Paterson, 2000b, ch. 2). Until the 1960s, Higher courses were intended primarily as a hurdle and a preparation for university, affecting only a very small minority of pupils, albeit with a backwash effect on the schooling of the majority. However, as an increasing number of pupils stayed in school beyond the compulsory years it was argued that the upper secondary system was failing the able and less able students alike (Tuck, 1999). The courses and qualifications in place were: Standard Grade followed by Highers (often covered as a 'two-term dash' in fifth or sixth year) and the Certificate of Sixth Year Studies (which was designed as a step towards mature independent study, but which was not formally recognised by the universities) along with the expedient of the National Certificate modules hastily introduced as a vocational strand. This comprised a patchy and unco-ordinated experi-ence for pupils, exhibiting curricular gaps and lack of progression. Highers suited those who had achieved three or more Credit level awards; pupils who had secured Standard Grade passes at General and Foundation levels arrived in fifth year and found no suitable courses which could take them forward and lead to progression beyond school. Changes in the entry requirements of the universities following the cuts of the 1980s made it necessary for many pupils to return after fifth year to upgrade their Highers, making Secondary 6 almost a 'remedial year' for some

(Raffe *et al.*, 2002). Revered as a national icon; recognised as an invaluable fixed point of secure academic standards; or regarded as symbolic of a destructive, over-assessed, competitive process – few educationalists were neutral in their views about what – if anything – should be done about 'the Highers'.

In 1990 the government set up a committee chaired by Professor John Howie with the remit of reviewing courses, assessment and certification in the fifth and sixth years – the two post-compulsory years – of secondary schooling (Secondary 5 and Secondary 6). Following the relatively recent efforts and upheavals which had accompanied the establishment of Standard Grade, Secondary 3 to Secondary 4 was regarded as a sacrosanct area which was not officially to be considered within the remit of the Howie Committee. However, as the group considered the coherence of secondary education and during the conception of *Higher Still*, proposals for developments which impinged on these years became inevitable, undoubtedly solving some of the problems, but introducing new and different anomalies from those existing previously (see Chapter 3).

The debate and Howie's proposals: ScotCert and ScotBac

What Scotland needs are more radical solutions than Scotland wants. (Howie, 1991, quoted in McPherson, 1992a, p. 127)

At the heart of the debate on the form, character and purposes of late secondary education were a wide range of issues of concern and import to different constituencies within the wider educational system. The one-year Higher was considered by some to lack breadth and depth, and to set lower standards of attainment either than English A levels or in the continental systems. Reduced to a 'two-term dash' it fostered a teacher-centred, transmission pedagogy and it was unsuitable for the wider range of young people then entering Secondary 5. Of particular concern to some was the extent to which specific changes such as the extension of Highers to two-year courses might Anglicise the system, and the extent to which any proposed changes might threaten the four-year degree of the Scottish universities. And there was the thorny issue of 'parity of esteem' between academic and vocational courses – was this desirable? Was it achievable?

As Paterson (2000b) indicates, Howie found areas of agreement on the general characteristics desirable at this stage for Scottish young people. The education experienced should be broad and deep, and should be flexible with respect to course structures and pathways. It should form links with both pre-16 education and with education and training beyond school, bridging the divide between academic and vocational study. It should encourage access to education, and staying on beyond 16 and 18. It should encourage those who left early to return. It should be efficient. 'And it should take account of the European dimension. This last was widely interpreted as code for: avoid the A-levels and look at models from elsewhere' (Paterson, 2000b, p. 61).

Although most of those who submitted views to the committee were of the view that change was needed for these aspirations to be fulfilled, all saw some merits in the existing system, and with so many different vested interests it was not surprising that there was little consensus on what changes should be implemented, most agreeing, however, that any changes should be evolutionary and incremental. The members of the Howie Committee firmly came to the conclusion that 'our system is seriously wanting in several respects' and that 'the status quo is not an option', but the changes they proposed were radical, clearly European, and immediately controversial.

The Howie Committee reported in 1992 (SOED, 1992) and in its proposals rejected both caution and incrementalism. Following a condensed Standard Grade completed over Secondary 2/3, a two-track system was proposed, comprising the Scottish Certificate (ScotCert) and the Scottish Baccalaureate (ScotBac) courses and qualifications. The former was to be modular, each Unit being individually and internally assessed, and covering academic subjects, core skills and vocational elements such as had already been established in the National Certificates. This track would cater for up to 60% of the cohort, last for up to two years and would be available in Further Education colleges as well as schools. It would end with a final external assessment. The second track, the ScotBac, which was modelled on similar French and Danish schemes, was to be mainly academic in character, cater for up to 40% of the cohort, and last for up to three years. Variants within it would have common core elements, but allow specific subjects to be studied well beyond the existing Higher levels. There would be assessment at the end of each year, but only the third and final of these would be external. Arrangements were suggested whereby pupils could transfer between the two tracks.

The proposals energised and radicalised the debate about upper secondary education. Again, although no consensus on a way forward emerged from the reactions in the wider educational constituency, there was fairly widespread agreement on two things – acceptance of the need for change and a decisive rejection of the divisive twin track system which Howie proposed (McPherson, 1992c; Paterson, 2000b).

The Inspectorate and the Scottish Upper Secondary Award (SUSA)

In 1993 the initiative passed back to the Inspectorate which had played a leading role in setting up the Howie Committee and in shaping its agenda. They attempted to create an alternative solution which would not only address the problems which had now been so publicly aired, but would also include the curriculum flexibility and the avoidance of tracking which had been signalled as important for acceptability throughout the educational community (Raffe *et al.*, 2002). They proposed the Scottish Upper Secondary Award (SUSA) – a model based on group awards. Each award would be achieved by taking a combination of courses derived from existing Highers and modules which would earn a specific volume and level of credit. The awards would be available at five levels each covering typically a year's study, and thus providing a progression ladder which students could start to climb at a level corresponding to their current attainments. Although not exemplifying any overall vision of education, the system had the merits of being pragmatic, logical and rational. It represented incremental change and incorporated, as much as reasonably could be accommodated, the basic specifications which any generally acceptable reform had to be seen to deliver.

Unfortunately, successful reform does not depend solely on logic and rationality. These proposals would have abolished the position of the Higher as the main currency of the Scottish secondary curriculum. Emotional and historical commitment to the Higher had been revitalised during the Howie debate. The SUSA proposal was too much for the Secretary of State, Ian Lang, who rejected a system based primarily on group awards. Whatever was to be devised in the name of more open accessibility and unhindered progression, the Higher as the benchmark of Scottish secondary education simply had to remain. This was the basis for the coded pun in the document issued by Ian Lang in 1994: *Higher Still: Opportunity for All* (Scottish Office, 1994). Bowing to traditionalists – the Higher would remain; bowing to politicians – standards were to be raised; bowing to the populace – social inclusion was to be advanced.

The characteristics of Higher Still *and the* New National Qualifications

> [Scottish education has placed] excessive emphasis upon the results of written examinations and has produced a class of people who combine an astonishing verbal facility with a meagre equipment of wisdom and little understanding of the complicated human situation and values involved in the words they so glibly use. (R. F. McKenzie quoted in Paterson, 2000b, p. 171)

Key elements in the *Higher Still* proposals were that there should be a single system of levels for both academic and vocational aspects of education, and that the arrangements for assessment should be the same. This meant that a merger between the two examining bodies, SCOTVEC and the Scottish Examination Board (SEB) with their distinctive certification systems was inevitable and by 1996 the Scottish Qualifications Authority (SQA) was formally established to oversee all external assessment arrangements in schools and Further Education (Tuck, 1999). The more interesting question was – which of the two distinctive assessment systems would be applied within the *Higher Still* courses? The answer that emerged, perhaps based on the politics of merger rather than on sound educational theory, good practice or common sense, appeared to be 'both'. This subsequently led to justifiable perceptions in the schools of an excessive assessment burden, and also brought the whole national qualification system to a chaotic halt.

Unlike the Standard Grade development, there had been no general debate associated with *Higher Still* on the philosophical basis of the curriculum and its relationship to wider cultural and educational ideals and contexts. Far from presenting a positive educational vision of a unified system – which was a radical new direction for post-16 education – the Inspectorate presented what appeared to many as no more than a 'technical fix' which addressed specific problems identified by the Howie Report and which was represented as an incremental and evolutionary process of improvement – a consolidation of ongoing reforms. Although like Standard Grade it could be described as an 'assessment-led' development, the assessment arrangements were not derived from a coherent model of linked curriculum and assessment principles which had been thoroughly worked over for each subject area by Joint Working Parties mainly comprising subject teachers as in the earlier development. The new arrangements appeared to represent only an administrative framework for the reorganisation of curriculum from two very different models and the unproblematic summative assessment and associated certification in a reasonably stepped series of levels and based on 40 hours of study.

The proposals incorporated many of the features of the SUSA model (which had close links with *The Action Plan* arrangements) but with a less central role for group awards. From 1999 the *Higher Still* reform introduced a 'unified system of courses and assessment' leading to National Qualifications (NQs) available at seven levels (Access 1 to Advanced Higher) with the aim of providing a unified 'climbing frame' that would enable all potential students, including lower-attaining 16 year-olds, to access provision at a suitable level and to have flexible opportunities to progress within the mainstream educational system (see Appendix 1). The previously existing academic qualifications, Highers and Certificate of Sixth Year Studies (CSYS) and the vocational National Certificate modules were replaced with New National Qualifications (NNQs), whose design rules for curriculum, assessment and certification were a hybrid of the SCOTVEC National Certificate module specification and internal assessment arrangements, and the formal processes and procedures of the then Scottish Exam Board's 'Conditions and Arrangements' for course content and meticulous external examination systems (Long, 1999). The building blocks of the new system were 40-hour modules – National Units – which could be taken as separate units or combined into 160-hour National Courses. Like the vocational modules of *The Action Plan*, each Unit was internally assessed; but to pass a course a student had to complete and pass three component modules or Units, and subsequently pass an external assessment, whose results alone – for most subjects – determined the final grade. Programmes of courses and Units which met specified criteria, including core skills, could lead to Scottish Group Awards (SGAs).

An additional contrast to the Standard Grade development were the reassurances given to teachers that the curriculum and assessment was not undergoing any radical change. In Standard Grade, the significant changes in the model of assessment had been extensively discussed and openly acknowledged as a vehicle for change in curriculum content and pedagogy – changes which many teachers welcomed. In the development of the NNQs, teachers were assured that the curriculum in many areas would not have to change – all that was required was simply the blocking of the learning periods into 40-hour units and the introduction of a more continuous and distributed timing of the assessment. Clearly these requirements fitted some subjects much more readily than others.

Although, as in other developments, there were contributions from a structure of committees which had broadly based representation from educational sectors and other relevant bodies, the development was rapidly driven forward by the Higher Still Development Unit (HSDU), which, although for administrative convenience was described as being located within the Scottish Consultative Council on the Curriculum (SCCC), actually reported directly to the administration within SOEID and the Inspectorate. Although a series of consultation documents were circulated and responded to concerning core skills, guidance, nomenclature, Access level provision and several other areas, no consultation paper on assessment and reporting was issued. The wider debate which was necessary on the principles and practical feasibility of the new assessment arrangements had no focus and did not take place in any co-ordinated fashion. The SCCC, which could have provided a focal point for debate, was advised that all papers relating to the decisions within the development committees and the HSDU processes were confidential and that the Council could be issued only with such information that came in due course into the public domain. Their urgently expressed reservations and concerns were dismissed as lightly as were the concerns of the Association of Directors of Education in Scotland (ADES), the EIS and other involved bodies. The general perception of an unresponsive, 'top-down' and disenfranchising initiative was well founded.

As in Standard Grade, the teaching profession baulked at the sudden escalation in teaching and assessment demands and, late in 1998, the EIS called for a boycott. Whereas under the same pressures the SCROAG Committee had substantially simplified the initial Standard Grade assessment requirements (see Chapter 3), the Liaison Group which was hastily convened to stem this growing wave of professional unrest brokered a deal whereby the implementation was to be staggered over five years from 1999 to 2004, with this phasing taking account of particular subjects on a school by school basis.

The assessment arrangements

The Howie Committee had explicitly rejected modularisation of the academic route of the ScotBac in the following terms:

> Modularisation can lead to fragmentation and trivialisation of learning. It can also be associated with over assessment and with assessment-driven learning. We realise, of course, that these problems can be overcome by imaginative course design which employs integration and linkage of modules. However, it may be argued that if a course is intended to be delivered as an integrated whole to a stable class group, there is no reason to disintegrate it in the first place. (SOED, 1992, p. 45)

The NNQ method of combining internal and external assessment is quite different from that of Standard Grade, in which internal assessment is applied to limited specific elements only (e.g. practical skills; talking) and the results of which contribute proportionally to the overall marks determining the final grade. Other on-going more informal internal assessments provide estimates which are used to support external awarding functions: prioritising scripts for quality assurance checks, identifying results which merit an appeal by providing reliable evidence of predictions etc. In contrast, within the NNQs system, internal assessments give teachers additional summative assessment responsibilities as these are a part of the award itself, requiring pupils to demonstrate competence or an acceptable level of understanding in all the learning outcomes of the course Units, in addition to preparing to demonstrate different kinds of attainment in the external assessments. However, candidates can be motivated by passing these periodic assessments, and those who fail are allowed a re-try, giving an opportunity for formative feedback.

In the external assessment the pupils are required to demonstrate the ability to retain, consolidate and, where appropriate, integrate the skills and knowledge acquired in the component Units. Although the candidate may be able to demonstrate achievement in these individual components at a particular time during the course, this does not necessarily mean that that he or she can demonstrate the required retention and integration of these at the end. As the assessment is also applied in a different context in the external and internal diets, there is also increased potential for a degree of mis-match and unreliability. There is an additional likelihood that the generally shortened external examination, by being able only to sample the work covered in the three component modules, will be an unreliable indicator of the student's overall work.

The requirements for a series of single Unit internal assessments placed huge additional demands on three areas of the system. Finally, one gave way in chaos. Firstly, modularisation dictates reliance on internal assessment because it is not feasible to assess externally a range of independent short components. This placed a significant new level of demand and responsibility on the teaching force. Secondly, the support to be given to teachers in their internal assessment came in the form of National Assessment Bank end-of-Unit assessment tests (NABs), which were assessment tasks or instruments which could be used to assess performance in a module. The initial production of these – on a wide scale (covering Units at 5 levels and in a wide range of subjects), to an acceptable standard and an appropriate timetable, placed huge demands on the HSDU. Finally, although the external examinations went smoothly, it was found difficult to secure enough markers and maintain the full complexity of the established quality assurance procedures which normally ensured the reliability and comparability expected of the national awards of the former Scottish Examination Board. Additionally, the administrative task of linking the final assessment grades with records of internal Unit passes from schools placed significant pressure on the administrative mechanisms of the new external examination body, the recently formed SQA.

The complexity and magnitude of this range of demands appear to have been completely underestimated by the Inspectorate, and despite the setting back of the initial implementation date to 1999, the whole edifice crashed in an unseemly public debacle in August of 2000 when the third link in the above chain, the administrative procedures of the external qualification awards failed to deliver the examination results the pupils and the teachers had worked so hard to secure. A full and detailed account of this event and its far reaching consequences for the Inspectorate and for the policy making mechanisms in Scottish education has been set out by Paterson (2000b) and Raffe *et al.* (2002).

This unseemly public failure and the continuing dissatisfaction expressed at the burden of assessment on both teachers and candidates prompted the Scottish Executive to mount a major review in 2001. The review (Scottish Executive, 2001b) confirmed the high demand of assessment and the confusion there had been among teachers over the role, nature and quality of NABs. Some teachers believed they did not stretch able pupils, and 50% considered that they did not adequately prepare students for the external assessment. The Review Group suggested that there were three key areas for improvement:

- to make the assessment more effective and efficient – by making purposes clearer and instruments sharper, and by spreading good practice;
- to reduce unnecessary duplication of effort – by avoiding assessing the same skills and knowledge more often than necessary;
- to reduce the burden of administration by streamlining processes.

These recommendations were accepted and a programme of subject and associated assessment reviews to address difficulties in these areas was initiated. However, the Review Group also suggested that while these actions would each have a positive impact, they might not be sufficient to resolve the key issue of the total burden of assessment. They suggested some design changes to the overall scheme might be considered, and offered two possible options. Option A would allow pupils to bypass Unit assessments and gain a course award from the external assessment only. Option B would allow students to receive ungraded course awards on the basis of Unit assessments only (Scottish Executive, 2001b, p. 29). These proposals were put out for consultation in September 2001. A majority of participants at consultation seminars opposed both options. Their reasons included the following: either of the options would increase workload and management tasks rather than reduce them; that it was too early to make changes to the new system; and that the suggested changes would imperil the principles of a unified system and parity of esteem. Clearly, despite the difficulties, the teachers were indicating that the status quo was now the preferred option thus reaffirming the general support expressed in many surveys to the basic principles of *Higher Still*.

What evidence is there on the success of Higher Still?

> The apparently rather odd conclusion, then, is that assessment, even though widely criticised for being invidious and excluding, has actually been a force for democratisation. (Paterson 2000b, p. 49)

Although Paterson was here referring to the period immediately prior to *Higher Still* in which Standard Grade and the National Certification had first begun to provide stepping stones by which a majority could, in principle, see Highers as potentially within their grasp, the comment could stand as an evaluation of the success of *Higher Still* and the NNQs. One of the central aims of *Higher Still* had been to extend 'opportunity for all' by providing access to mainstream qualifications at several levels connected by a single progression framework. A formal research study of *Higher Still* in practice was undertaken by the Centre for Educational Sociology (CES) at the University of Edinburgh. Survey data from schools, teachers and pupils; qualitative and quantitative data from school case studies; and analysis of SQA data on all NNQ candidates during the first three years of implementation; provided information on the attainment of the aims to extend access to the full range of the curriculum, to raise levels of attainment, and to ensure equity and parity of esteem across courses. Raffe (2003) concludes that despite a mixed verdict on some aspects of its performance, Scottish Education is improving. 'Attainments have risen at all levels. Full time participation has increased, especially in the fifth and sixth years of school and in HE where participation rates more than doubled within a decade' (p. 797).

With respect to raising attainment, Paterson (2000b) has pointed out that the proportions of pupils attaining specific qualifications had been steadily rising since 1965. Rates of staying on beyond 16 – a function of the formal raising of the school leaving age and of youth employment prospects – had reached three-quarters in the late 1990s, up from just over half in the 1980s, and from just over one-third in the late 1970s. The proportion of school leavers with at least one Higher grade pass had reached 44% in 1998, just before the introduction of *Higher Still*. The proportion with three or more passes – informally the threshold for entry to university – had reached 30%, up from 23% in 1989, from 20% in 1980, and from 12% in 1965. 'In fact, in 1998 a higher proportion of the age group was reaching this university-entrance level than had been scraping just one O-Grade in 1965. At the same time, research commissioned by the Scottish Office had shown that the standards of the Highers had remained broadly intact' (p. 60).

The CES analysis of SQA data showed this upward trend continuing. Students entering Secondary 5 with middle and low Standard Grade attainments – students who previously would have struggled to attain any Highers – attempted more courses than before at appropriate levels and increased their total volume of SQA certificated study. The new levels introduced by *Higher Still* were seen to have higher standing than the provision they replaced and they provided a more worthwhile learning experience (Raffe *et al.*, 2005). The data presented by SQA staff (De Luca, 2003) show that with respect to Highers, there has been an improved performance overall since 1987, particularly with an increase in pupils passing three or more Highers. However, at the other end of the attainment spectrum, the size of the attainment gains have not been as great and middle and lower attaining 16 year-olds continue to lag behind in attainment in comparison with pupils at the same levels in many other countries (see Chapter 5). Mere provision of mechanisms for unimpeded progression is clearly not sufficient for narrowing the attainment gap between highest and lowest attainers.

The data indicates that an acknowledged success of Higher Still was the inclusion of students with learning difficulties within the mainstream curriculum and qualifications systems (Raffe *et al.*, 2005). Staff in special and mainstream schools thought that Higher Still had succeeded in giving such students access to the national curriculum at an appropriate level, the opportunity for national certification of their learning and better progression possibilities than had been available previously (Howieson *et al.*, 2005).

The data from the SQA and other studies with respect to gender differences in attainment in the NNQs are similar to those reported for Standard Grade (see Chapter 3). At Higher, as for Standard Grade, females continue to outperform male candidates. More stay on to attempt more Highers and they achieve more passes, particularly at the 3+ Highers level. In 2001, 21% of males within the age group achieved this level of qualification at the end of Secondary 5, while the corresponding figure for the females was 29% (De Luca, 2003). This gap has shown little sign of closing from 1987, and has clearly been unaffected by the introduction of qualifications built on incremental steps. Several respondents in a recent set of case studies in secondary schools indicated their belief that the differences between males and females was reduced in Secondary 5/6 as males became more mature and caught up with the females in terms of attainment. Analysis of the Scottish School Leavers Survey appear to support this perception, but only for those males who had attained one or more credit level passes at Standard Grade (Croxford *et al.*, 2003).

The future of the National Qualifications

The Ministerial Response to *A Curriculum for Excellence* indicates the need for 'a broader range of outcomes in line with the purposes of *A Curriculum for Excellence*' and reaffirms the process of on-going review of the NNQ 'to update them and improve them over time' (Scottish Executive, 2004d). In those schools which have moved Standard Grade to Secondary 2/3 there are moves to revitalise and extend vocational education in the middle and upper stages, since within schools the vocational element has continued to have a low profile and priority in comparison with the longer established, traditional academic strands. However, unlike England, the political climate in Scotland is supportive of a unified system. Perhaps new courses, developed in partnership with the Further Education colleges, will advance the concept of 'parity of esteem' between vocational and academic education in schools that *Higher Still* took the first ambitious steps to introduce.

CHAPTER 5

NATIONAL AND INTERNATIONAL MONITORING

Here's tae us, wha's like us?

As Michael Forsyth had indicated in the 1987 curriculum and assessment paper (see Chapter 2), the Scots have indeed long felt proud of their educational system. Have we not got the most highly qualified and professionally developed teachers and the most meticulously organised and objective external examination system in the world? And had we not exported our models of teaching, the structure of curriculum and the organisation of schools to grateful British colonies around the world?

But was our continuing belief in our superiority justifiable? While we rested on our laurels, the rest of the world might well have caught up – and perhaps even surpassed us. In 1996 the results of the Third International Mathematics and Science Survey (TIMSS) generated an international league table of pupil attainment in aspects of mathematics and science across 39 countries which suggested to some that we might just have become a wee bit complacent. The then Director of the Scottish Council for Research in Education (SCRE) described the results as 'the cause of an unpleasant shiver down the Scottish spine' (Harlen, 1997). If we are to be secure in our conviction that we have a first class educational system, how much credence should we put on the evidence from studies such as these? How comparable is the international data to those from the Scottish in-house monitoring of standards? Do such studies provide assessment evidence we can rely on to provide guidance on improvement? Or do the outcomes merely prompt shock press headlines and ineffective, political 'quick fixes' for complex educational problems?

The international comparative studies: TIMSS, PISA and PIRLS
The emergence and growth of the global economy and the perception by governments of the importance of key workforce skills in mathematics and science as critical precursors to economic progress have led countries increasingly to seek information not only on what their school-age populations know and can do in these key subjects, but also to seek

perspectives on what other nations – particularly potential economic competitors – with similar or different educational practices are achieving (e.g. see NCES, 2003). The most systematic international studies which offer comparative data on pupil attainment across countries are associated with the International Association for Evaluation of Educational Achievement (IEA), an organisation which has its administrative head-quarters in the Netherlands (for details see www.iea.nl). Since the early 1960s it has undertaken the co-ordination of internationally comparative studies 'designed to provide policy makers, educators, researchers and practitioners with information about educational achievement and learning contexts'. Increasingly, as the interest of governments in comparative data on attainment has grown, additional countries have contracted to join, each country funding its own participation and contributing to the costs of co-ordinating the studies internationally. Centres with particular expertise contribute appropriately as partners in the different studies, for example the International Study Center, Boston College (management of the studies); National Foundation for Educational Research, England (test development); Statistics Canada (sampling design).

As in all activities involving testing, ways of defining the subject domains have to be agreed and be seen to be educationally and conceptually sound. As educational practices and goals change over time, these domains too have been evolving in the studies, making backward comparisons somewhat more difficult. But as each study cycle has developed, the techniques for test construction, data gathering and management have been subjected to more refinement and checking to ensure quality outcomes. Countries must meet rigorous standards for sampling and applying procedures designed to give appropriate representation in order to prevent bias and to ensure comparability. Translating the tests and questionnaires involve increasingly sophisticated, iterative review processes, and numerous training sessions and checks are held to ensure data collection and scoring procedures are standardised to give optimal consistency and comparability across countries (Goldstein, 1996; Adams, 2003).

The main IEA surveys in which Scotland has participated are TIMSS and PIRLS which we explore below, in addition to the PISA survey which is mounted under the auspices of the Organisation for Economic Co-operation and Development (OECD) (see www.pisa.oecd.org).

The Third International Mathematics and Science Survey (TIMSS)

Scotland participated in the first mathematics (1964) and science (1971) surveys, in the second mathematics survey in the late 1980s, and the third mathematics and science studies in 1995 (TIMSS, 1999). The development of the framework for the assessment in the two subject areas involved widespread participation and reviews by educators around the world. A key overall requirement of the frameworks was that they included goals of mathematics and science education regarded as important in a significant number of participating countries. In the third study, in addition to the attainment tests applied to more than half a million pupils after 4 and 8 years of schooling in over 40 countries, questionnaires for pupils and headteachers were designed to gather data on contextual factors in policy relevant areas, and also provided the basis for producing internationally significant research. Since the studies provide large data sets from securely sampled sources, researchers across the world are subsequently able to use these to undertake detailed explorations of relationships, for example between pupil performance and educational resources and class size (Woessmann and West, 2002). TIMSS has continued with a 2003 survey designated the Trends in International Mathematics and Science Study (TIMSS, 2004).

The 1995 survey data seemed to indicate that, notwithstanding the relatively large classes, and apparently undifferentiated whole-class teaching methods of countries such as Japan and South Korea, these frequently appeared in the top five performers in the league tables. Subsequently, additional research was initiated in the form of videotape studies with the aim of providing a rich source of information regarding the teaching and learning contexts of eighth grade mathematics classrooms, and comparing the observed teaching practices with some of the reform documents – and teachers' perceptions of their recommendations – which had resulted from the earlier studies (Stigler and Hiebert, 1999). Japan had performed particularly well; the US, lower than the average country in performance in mathematics, had found its national goal to be 'first in the world in science and mathematics achievement by the year 2000' not even approximated (NPACI, 1998); and Germany reacted particularly badly to their pupils' relatively poor performances (Prenzel and Duit, 2000). These three countries participated in the first videotape study; an additional five (excluding Scotland) have joined the repeat video study due to be completed in 2004 (TIMSS, 1998). Additional features continue to be added to the studies. The TIMSS 2003 survey gathered data on the educational levels of parents, and published each country's 'Human Development Index' – the national equivalent of the 'socio-economic status' of the catchment area of a school – a statistic which incorporates information such as life expectancy and gross national income per capita. TIMSS 2003 data are currently being evaluated by the participating countries and other interested bodies such as the World Bank (TIMSS, 2004; Gilmore, 2005). Meanwhile, preparation and item-writing for the 2007 survey are well under way.

Programme for International Student Assessment (PISA)

The PISA studies were set up by the OECD to run in three-yearly cycles from 2000 to assess not so much pupils' specific attainments vis-à-vis the typical school curricula as in TIMSS but, rather more ambitiously, to assess

> how well young adults near the end of compulsory schooling are prepared to meet the challenges of today's knowledge societies. PISA is forward looking, focussing on young people's ability to reflect on and apply their knowledge and skills to meet the challenges of adult life in the real world.

The tests are designed for pupils towards the end of their compulsory schooling (age 15–16 years) and are organised around three domains: mathematical literacy, scientific literacy and reading literacy:

> The preconditions for independent, life-long and co-operative learning as well as problem solving competencies and aspects of communication and co-operation are assessed. (OECD, 2003; Adams, 2003)

Like the TIMSS studies, the PISA study involves the completion of questionnaires by the headteacher of participating schools and by the pupils, in addition to the completion of pupil tests. National demographic data, family and student characteristics and school qualities were also incorporated in 2003.

The PISA study in 2000, which involved 32 countries, was the first major international assessment where, in addition to the typical multiple-choice items, 55% of the tasks were constructed response items. While some of these required little judgement on the markers' part, others requiring reflection or interpretation were clearly more vulnerable to marker variability. Marking guides were designed to reduce this as far as possible, and scoring codes constructed for full or partial credit. Scotland took part in the study in 2000 and 2003 (Thorpe, 2004) and will also participate in PISA 2006.

Progress in International Reading Literacy Study (PIRLS)

This is the most recently developed of the IEA's studies, with 35 countries, including Scotland, participating in the first study in 2001. While PISA assesses end-of-schooling literacy, PIRLS assesses a range of reading comprehension strategies for two major reading purposes – literary and informational at ages 9–10 years. More than half of the items were in the constructed response format rather than the objective multiple choice format, requiring students to generate their own answers. Examples of passages and marking guides can be found in PIRLS (2001). Because of the recognition that the home, school and national context within which children learn to read play such important roles, PIRLS questionnaires collected extensive information about aspects of these factors. Not only did pupils complete questions on their home and school experiences of learning to read, their parents and caregivers also gave information on activities used to foster early literacy activities. The next study will be in 2006.

The findings of the international comparative studies

If Standard Grade and Highers are high stakes testing for pupils, and 5–14 test outcomes for their classes are high stakes testing for teachers, then there is no doubt that the results of the international surveys are high stakes testing for the policy makers. With respect to the TIMSS findings, the newspaper headlines were always the first to break the news to most Scots: 'Eurodunce?' asked *Scotland on Sunday* in 1992 (Briggs, 1992); 'Scots pupils lag behind in maths and science' the *Scotsman* informed the public in 1997 (Wells, 1997). Certainly, by judicious and selective reporting, the press could and did generate depressing reading but the selective and diverse interpretations of results have clearly been shaped by the purposes and intentions of those reporting. Certainly, it has not all been doom and gloom, but there have been many prompts for thought and national reflection.

The aggregation of data into one figure and subsequent ranking of countries masks the minutiae of differences in the many fascinating and detailed sub-sets of data published in the different survey reports. The most reassuring findings for Scottish educators are derived from the recent PISA statistics collected primarily from OECD countries (Thorpe, 2004). While the top performers in scientific literacy were found in Finland, Japan and Korea, Scottish 15-year-olds performed reassuringly above the average. However, in contrast to many of these top performing countries, Scottish data showed a concerningly wide spread of scores between the highest and lowest attainers. There was also a fairly positive picture of Scotland with respect to pupil proficiency in both mathematics and reading with mean scores comfortably above the average. With respect to the TIMSS 2004 study, Thorpe reported that

> the results show that our performance in mathematics is not significantly different from the international average at P5 but is significantly higher than this average at S2. In science, our performance was significantly above the international average at both P5 and S2. (p. 6)

Thorpe points to the differences between the curriculum and test construction approaches of the TIMSS and the PISA surveys as being the basis of the discrepancies between their data.

The findings of the PIRLS 2001 study of fourth grade reading achievement indicated clearly the association between the acquisition of literacy and economic and home factors. However, while generally reassuring, PIRLS data set Scotland lower than England in attainment levels of reading for the 9-year-olds. The TIMSS data has always been the least reassuring for the Scottish educators. The early data for 12/13-year-olds indicated that Scottish pupil attainment scores hovered about the average for 46 countries, with a relatively low proportion attaining the high and advanced benchmark scores. The scores of the 11-year-olds lagged considerably behind those of England.

Setting aside comparisons with other countries, the most reliable assessment of national standards could clearly be obtained through a study which was born and bred in Scotland, designed and tailored for the particular ages and stages of Scottish schools and framed within the Scottish curriculum. There was just such a study in the form of the Assessment of Achievement Programme.

The national monitoring system: the Assessment of Achievement Programme (AAP) and the Scottish Survey of Achievement (SSA)

The Conservative government of the 1980s had been keenly aware that any proposed policy change in curriculum or practices within schools needed the leverage of sound evidence on standards of pupil attainment. Were attainment levels low or high relative to professional or popular claims? Were they rising or falling? Clearly, for informed debate and sound policy making, the systematic collection of objective and reliable data on what pupils actually knew and could do at key stages in Scottish schools was required.

In the early 1980s the Assessment of Achievement Programme was set up and since then has been attempting to provide reliable answers to questions such as these. It was initially informed by the experiences and work of English researchers in the Assessment of Performance Unit (APU) (see Murphy, 1990) and the detail of the early domain definitions and content were determined by reference to policy documents and the views of the profession. The remit of the AAP surveys was to:

- provide a picture of performance levels of pupils at certain stages;
- gather evidence of any change in performance over time;
- provide feedback to education authorities, curriculum developers and teachers which would contribute to the improvement of learning and teaching.

The pupils tested by AAP were at stages Primary 4, Primary 7 and Secondary 2, and comprised a random sample of around 2% of these pupil age groups. To meet the first of these aims, the assessment items must reflect the curriculum which pupils experience at different ages and stages, and the expectancy of appropriate levels of attainment across these must be defined. As the curriculum changes, so must the content of the tests and the management of the data. However, in order to achieve the second aim, there must be some degree of continuity over the years of the cycles, for example in specific test items, methodology and sampling procedures. The first rounds of data collection concerned mathematics (1983), English language (1984) and science (1987). Surveys in these three subjects have continued in staggered three- to four-year cycles until the present and until 1996 were treated as research projects in their funding and management procedures. Full details of the surveys, their processes and key findings can be found in Stark *et al.*(1997); Stark (1999); Condie *et al.* (2003) and Wilson (2003).

The Scottish Education Department press release dealing with the results of the 1988 mathematics survey which appeared to show a deteriorating performance at Primary 4 and Primary 7 since 1983, was seen by some educationalists as the rationale for advancing the Conservative Party political agenda in ways that were inimical to the teaching profession: 'Michael Forsyth seized on these conclusions to support his plans for National Testing and a national curriculum in the primary schools. National Testing and teacher appraisals are now provisions in the Self-Governing Schools Etc. (Scotland) Bill' (McPherson, 1989). McPherson then proceeded in his article to question the reliability of the findings of the study as a consequence of a perceived lack of continuity particularly in the technicalities of the methodology and sampling.

Since then many potential sources of technical unreliability have been systematically dealt with by the research teams and the Central Support Unit at SCRE which was commissioned to advise on and rationalise the sampling procedures, and from around 1994 the tests and the reporting of findings have increasingly been in terms of the 5–14 curriculum. In 1996 a national co-ordinator was appointed at the Scottish Office to oversee and manage all the surveys, with subject expertise contracted as considered necessary. Since then the surveys have provided the most reliable vehicle for the central monitoring of national standards, in contrast to the inappropriate use of the National Tests for this purpose (see Chapter 2). For example, the AAP results of the sixth survey of English language (SEED, 2003) were consistent with the findings from HMI Inspection reports that the nationally defined 5–14 levels for reading were reached by 63% in Primary 4, but by only 41% in Primary 7 and 43% in Secondary 2, whereas the results of National Testing reported by schools reported significantly higher figures (81%, 72% and 61% respectively for the three pupil groups). Overly narrow sampling of the domain in National Tests, teaching to the test, and other features of the classroom testing context almost certainly contributed to these discrepancies. The report of the sixth science AAP survey (SEED, 2005b) reaffirmed the fall in science interest and motivation through Primary 7 to Secondary 2, and little or no improvement in levels of attainment despite the introduction of revised 5–14 guidelines in 2000.

In future, national attainment will be monitored exclusively by a revamped AAP in the form of the Scottish Survey of Achievement (SSA) (see www.ltscotland.org.uk/assess/of/ssa_gen.asp):

From May 2005 [we will] introduce a new Scottish Survey of Achievement. This will build upon the more limited AAP. It will use a representative sampling approach to assess pupils' attainments and provide an overview of attainment levels in each educational Authority and at national level. (Scottish Executive, 2004b)

The new extended survey thus separates national monitoring completely from classroom assessments and National Assessments (see Chapter 1) and will cover the key areas of the curriculum and core skills in the context of each key area, beginning with English language in 2005 and continuing in a four-year cycle to include initially mathematics, science and social subjects. Wider sampling than previously in half of the Authorities seriatim, will enable these to be monitored and reported on in each round, and key sub-groups such as 'vulnerable' pupil groups can also be identified. From 2006 the Survey results will also be linked to information from the international surveys.

The implications of survey outcomes for policy
As MacBeath notes, among the immediate effects of the international survey reporting are

> inflows and outflows of educational travellers in search of the ingre-
> dients that put a country at the top of the league table. While previous
> sites of educational cherry picking were Japan and Taiwan, interest
> has now turned to Finland and Korea which topped the 2001 PISA
> table. What such research studiedly ignores is that achievement rests
> primarily not on what happens in schools and classrooms but what
> happens outside them. (MacBeath, 2003, p. 804; see also PISA
> Newsletter, 2004 for some reactions)

Only comparative studies such as that of educational systems in Denmark, England and France (Osborn *et al.*, 2003) can illuminate the richness of national culture, values, practices and attitudes which impinge on the young, leading to diverse learning experiences, even when the curriculum superficially appears similar.

Although such surveys cannot identify even relatively simple cause and effect relationships and findings must be treated with caution (Goldstein, 2004), the data can be used to support the findings from other internal data sources – in Scotland these primarily comprise the AAP findings and the qualitative data from inspectorate reports. In some countries government responses included quite stringent requirements for targeted changes, for example in England the National Literacy and Numeracy Strategies. In Scotland, the literacy advice was more general, and less authoritarian, with central government simply advising and supporting Authorities in mounting their own literacy initiatives. National policy initiatives on homework and truancy were responses to the TIMSS results which indicated that 'more pupils were absent in a typical day in Scotland than in any other country; less homework was set in mathematics and in science than in almost all other countries' (both primary and secondary). The regular AAP findings of the relatively flat progress of pupils from Primary 7 to Secondary 2 in science has been the subject of many ineffective but continuing initiatives to revitalise the vital early secondary years of this subject (HMIE, 2005). The long tail of low attainment has also been a focus for Executive action. The PIRLS 2001 results, placing the Scottish performance in reading below that of England will have raised the question in the minds of some as to whether there should have been an alternative national literacy strategy, or whether in Scotland, specific pedagogical or cultural factors are negatively influential on reading levels.

The implications of survey outcomes for practice

The international and national survey data give the government useful information on the general level of performance of the educational system, prompting useful debate concerning the possible causal relationships among the contributing variables. However, while critical in a relatively uninformed way of the processes of the surveys, Authority staff and teachers remain relatively indifferent to the findings and possible implications for practice of the these surveys – so much so that teachers in England failed to respond to requests for involvement, resulting in the exclusion of England from the main PISA report of 2003. Nevertheless, the third aim of the AAP initiatives was to provide feedback directly to teachers in order to inform practitioner-based initiatives for improvement. The feedback took the form of Newsletters and booklets in which key areas of difficulty were illustrated and questions were raised on which teachers were invited to reflect: 'Is the apparent lack of conceptual understanding of percentages an area of concern for teachers? What teaching approaches could be used to deal with this?' (AAP, 1993). 'Are you aware of the need to go beyond simple question and answer routines to uncover pupil misconceptions?' (AAP, 1995). However, the continuing poor performance of pupils according to the TIMSS outcomes in 1996 along with the AAP in mathematics findings were strongly influential in the more pointed recommendations made by HMI in 1997 for changes to be made to practice in schools and pre-service education. *Improving Mathematics Education 5–14* (HMI, 1997) recommended, amongst other things, 'setting' or 'broad banding' in secondary schools, and more direct and interactive whole class teaching in both sectors. The recommendations appeared to be an amalgam of conventional conceptions of 'good practice' and 'what should work' from the profession (particularly HMI) and the techniques apparently associated with success in the high performing countries such as Japan.

But what actually does work? The year 1997 also saw the publication of the findings of a research study into the activities of primary teachers in England who appeared to be promoting highly effective numeracy skills in their pupils. The researchers found they had identified teachers who were themselves proactive in generating and engaging with the kinds of questions raised in the AAP booklets. They had subsequently pursued self-directed professional development through 'mutual support independent of unsympathetic colleagues', and read research on mathematics education to aid reflection before planning their collaborative developments (Askew *et al.*, 1997; *Times Educational Supplement Scotland*, 1997a). This contrasts with the approach of Scottish teachers who appeared to seek improvement through asking for external provision of improved training on managing individualised schemes, more textbooks, more accurate grading strategies, and advice on timely pupil setting (*Times Educational Supplement Scotland*, 1997b). While the English teachers appeared to have adopted a proactive collaborative enquiry engagement with professional learning, the Scottish profession appears to have sought directives from external 'experts' through a transmission mode familiar to all in Scottish education, and known to be largely ineffective (see Chapter 7).

CHAPTER 6

DIAGNOSTIC AND FORMATIVE ASSESSMENT

To incorporate formative assessment into their teaching would involve teachers in far more than acquisition of the necessary skills. Their view of the aims of the teaching of their own subject might have to change if they are to be close to their students in guiding them. The changes in classroom practice might also involve profound changes of role, even for teachers regarded by themselves and others as already successful. (Black, 1993, p. 79)

Introduction

In the concluding paragraphs of his review of *Formative and Summative Assessment by Teachers*, Black (1993) identified three necessary advances if formative assessment was to be properly developed in schools and make the powerful contribution of which it is potentially capable to increasing the effectiveness of learning:

- public and political action to establish the systems, contexts and the understandings needed for the survival of development and innovation;
- investment in research and development to extend and exploit the new possibilities for developing pupils' learning potential that recent work has opened up;
- development work with teachers to change the understandings and roles of both teachers and pupils and embed formative assessment in learning programmes.

There is a complex and extremely convoluted relationship between policy, research and practice and, over the past twenty years, policy aspirations, research findings and classroom activities have interacted productively to change both the concept of formative assessment and the model of the translation of policy into effective and enduring classroom practices. Within the Scottish Office and the Scottish Executive there have been policy makers who held the conviction that that the concept of

formative assessment and its development into practical classroom procedures were crucial factors in promoting quality in learning and teaching
and who tried to maintain its profile throughout the years when summative assessment absorbed most of the attention and energies of the
political and professional communities. Research stimulated debate and
the extension and refinement of both the concept and the means by which
it might be brought into effective practice. Through policy-initiated
dissemination of research findings and their implications, school-based
initiatives were prompted, and understanding and acceptance of formative assessment as an integral component of learning and teaching
permeated throughout the teaching force. However, for knowledge and
understanding to be more than inert academic knowledge or professional
rhetoric, it must be transformed into effective practices which are a
comfortable part of the individual teacher's repertoire and suited to the
context – the teaching aims, the pupil characteristics and the subject-
matter. Real change at the intimate interface of teacher and learner
interactions is the most difficult to achieve.

It is perhaps useful to deal with the evolution of formative assessment
in Scotland in terms of two different phases. Characteristic of the first
phase (the late 1970s until the mid 1990s) were the attempts of policy
makers to promote change in classroom practice through the dissemination of research findings and exemplification of practice in centrally
developed materials. In the second and currently ongoing phase, the focus
has moved to an exploration of how key aspects of formative assessment
shown by research to be effective can be developed and customised by
teachers themselves into practices which they consider to be effective in
supporting learning. Meanwhile, throughout both of these phases, the
concept of formative assessment has been evolving and changing.

Phase 1: Policy, research and practice: the cascade model

Developments associated with Standard Grade

> It is insufficient to devise curricular objectives and to find out if they
> have been attained by each pupil; for those who are not successful the
> reasons for misunderstandings require to be identified and alternative
> methods adopted. (SED, 1977b, The Dunning Report)

In the mid 1970s, the Dunning Committee's report, *Assessment for All*,
first introduced many in the educational community to the idea that
assessment might serve purposes other than merely sorting pupils. They
suggested that the new system of criterion referencing (see Chapter 3)
should not only be regarded as a replacement for norm referencing as a
method of judging pupils' progress against intended outcomes, but also as
a means of contributing to the improvement of educational attainment –
learning difficulties could be identified and instructional action could

then be taken when pupils failed to reach specified attainments. The thinking of the policy makers at this time was influenced by Benjamin Bloom's work on mastery learning and the concept of alterable variables in the learning context, and by Popham (1973), the leading exponent of criterion-referenced assessment in America, who argued that the introduction of this new form of assessment would have little to recommend it if it was not used as a springboard to improved instructional quality. Additionally, the *Pupils in Profile* project (SCRE, 1977) commissioned by the Headteachers' Association of Scotland, had piloted ways of describing pupils' achievements and influenced the thinking of the Dunning Committee that teachers' professional judgements, suitably moderated, would be an essential component of assessment for certification of abilities which could not be covered in an examination.

Although the recommendation of Dunning appeared both reasonable and sensible, there was at that time a lack of clarity both in theory and practice on how this form of diagnostic assessment might operate. Was it the case that tests which were criterion referenced to intended outcomes could serve not only the summative function of giving an account of what pupils had learned, but also diagnose learning difficulties? And what particular instructional action should be taken following pupil failure? In some subjects, notably science and mathematics, 'remedial loops' had already been incorporated into instructional materials but many teachers found these difficult to incorporate into the lock-step delivery which was typical of the time, and there was no convincing evidence that the pre-set remedial activities actually addressed the learning difficulties experienced by the individual pupil within the particular learning task in hand. Clearly, considerably more work was needed to inform any changes in practice.

In response to the Dunning Report's suggestion that 'diagnostic assessment as an aid to pupil learning' should be further investigated, the research community in Scotland embarked enthusiastically on a programme of exploration largely funded by the Scottish Office, and by 1983 a full edition of the journal *Programmed Learning and Educational Technology* under the guest editor, Harry Black, was devoted to research reports of a range of initiatives (Black, 1983). Within the wide-ranging papers, the key difficulties were identified and discussed: the time and effort required for significant change to take place in teachers' thinking and practice; resolution of the tensions in the relationship between formative and summative assessment; the identification of ways of successfully introducing innovation; the complexity of the professional context within which the changes were to take place; and the reconceptualisation of the nature of pupil learning difficulties and professionally appropriate ways of dealing with them. All the developments since then, including the most recent AifL initiatives (L&T Scotland, 2003) have been wrestling with these very significant problems.

Initially it was debated whether criterion-referenced assessment which identified particular areas of pupil failure might be sufficiently informative to point towards appropriate teacher action. Subsequently, designated 'diagnostic assessment', the process acquired overtones of a medical model. Pupils' learning failures were treated as signs of pathology in the learning process and investigations were considered necessary to diagnose the nature of the learners' difficulties. The identification of the intended outcomes of the learning activities and of the current knowledge and understanding of pupils – including their misconceptions – were seen as key components of this investigative activity. These processes and the subsequent pedagogic responses to the identified specific difficulties and needs of the pupils rather than the application of test items were beginning to be seen as central to the formative assessment process (Simpson and Arnold, 1984).

HMI Ernie Spencer in his 1987 paper *Assessment as Part of Teaching* (Spencer, 1987) further eased the concept away from its association with tests of any kind, setting out for secondary teachers the idea that the processes of formative assessment rested in the activities of the teacher responding sensitively to the existing knowledge and needs of learners as they engaged with a school learning task, rather than being vested solely in the application of a set of test items. Practical support took the form of a package containing printed advice about *Assessment as Part of Teaching* and a videotape, developed by Eric Drever and colleagues at the University of Stirling, with an accompanying commentary illustrating this type of assessment in action in a number of secondary subjects. A particular feature of the presentation of this material was that no technical terms were used since it was considered that the varying interpretations which might be put on such terms as 'formative', 'diagnostic' and 'summative' would create confusion and that their use would reinforce the teachers' tendency to believe that formative assessment is a complex, difficult matter requiring specialist academic expertise well beyond the normal teaching skills. However, in the secondary sector, where all curriculum and teaching developments were dominated by the new summative external subject examinations, formative practices made little headway and end-of-section tests remained the norm.

Developments associated with the 5–14 development programme

> The Government believes that every pupil should benefit from a properly structured programme of assessment which is part of the process of learning and teaching . . . It will be a key aim of the programme that teachers should be supplied with adequate guidance on teaching the curriculum and on assessment. (SED, 1987)

In the late 1980s the assessment procedures throughout the primary sector and in the first two years of secondary were highlighted as a priority area for reform and the formative aspect of assessment was again given place in the consultation document that initiated the reforms. In the *5–14 Assessment Guidelines* which were subsequently developed as part of the promised guidance (SOED, 1991), assessment was deliberately set within a framework which was familiar to teachers in order to build on and develop further the established skills and procedures of the profession. The framework comprised the following cycle of elements: **planning**: *(knowing and sharing what is to be learned)*; **teaching**: *(assessment as part of effective learning and teaching)*; **recording**: *(summarising success and progress)*; **reporting**: *(providing useful feedback)* and **evaluating**: *(using assessment to evaluate learning and teaching)*. There is clear evidence here and in the accompanying texts of the promotion of the key elements of formative assessment as being embedded in effective teaching strategies. However, the promotion of the idea that the National Tests should be used to assist teachers to inform their perceptions of children's progress pushed the debate about diagnostic assessment back to the consideration of formal assessments.

In both the 5–14 Assessment and the National Testing documents the 'technical jargon' of assessment procedures was once again eschewed. Nevertheless, the terminology had clearly penetrated the vocabulary of teachers to the extent that the National Tests, which were produced at the same time and dominated all 5–14 related discussions, were publicly and vociferously rejected by the teaching profession on the grounds that they were not 'diagnostic' and could not therefore be used to use to inform teaching (see Chapter 2). The teachers claimed that they could only be used summatively and could add nothing to what teachers already knew. Hitherto, any tests which teachers had applied had not been designed to inform instruction and, although they claimed that their ongoing observations of pupils' attainments and difficulties were well-established, informal forms of assessment used in a routine way to inform the teaching process, because these activities were intuitive, unsystematic and unrecorded, they went largely unexamined and unevaluated. The relationship between tests used diagnostically to identify learning failures and formative assessment as specific strategies embedded in effective teaching again became confused and unresolved.

Rumour has it that the Minister for Education in Scotland, not unreasonably, asked to be shown some 'diagnostic tests'. Despite the claims of the teaching profession that formative or diagnostic assessment procedures were part of their normal repertoire, there was at this stage little concrete exemplification which they could offer to illustrate the difference between systematic assessment or teachers' assessment strategies which were appropriate to the support of learning and those practices which solely measured in a summative manner the outcomes of teaching. This public demonstration of the non-existence of written assessments or systematic activities planned and devised for this purpose and related to the curriculum served to fuel further debate on whether diagnosis of learning difficulties could indeed be effected by some form of assessment instrument or whether it was more properly thought of as one of the complex interactive processes of teaching.

The powers of persuasion of those within the Scottish Office Education Department who were committed to assessment as a process to support the learning of pupils again prevailed and government funding was subsequently allocated for the development of teacher support materials under the generic title of *Taking a Closer Look* which illustrated practical procedures suitable for use in classrooms for the promotion of formative activities in mathematics, reading, writing and science. These were developed through the collaboration of teacher trainers, researchers and HMI and were made available to all schools in the autumn of 1995 (for example, Hayward and Hall, 1995). In these support materials the principles of the *5–14 Assessment Guidelines* were reaffirmed, and classroom strategies were described for looking more closely at pupils' ongoing work and questioning pupils to gain insights into their thinking and understanding.

The impact on practice

As an outcome of the early research activities a variety of different types of publications and resources had been produced for teachers (e.g. Black and Dockrell, 1984; Simpson and Arnold, 1984) which were promoted through in-service and teachers' conferences, stimulating considerable interest and debate among teachers on the different forms which classroom assessment might take, what purposes these might serve, and under what conditions teachers might find it possible to engage effectively and productively in the application of processes which investigated and responded to pupil difficulties and barriers to learning. The 'quality indicators' used by the Schools' Inspectorate to evaluate the performances of schools and the quality of experiences offered, included some indicators specifying formative uses of assessment. All schools therefore had become aware of these requirements in the formal national inspection programme and of the kinds of practices which could illustrate that the requirements are being met.

What consequently developed in the thinking and practices of teachers? It is difficult to quantify the extent of change since formative assessment can take a variety of forms in different contexts and is only reliably identified at the intimate interface of teaching and learning. However, there were a few positive indications of change at a number of levels. In the secondary schools the technical jargon at least had clearly entered the vocabulary of many of the staff: in a national survey in late 1996, 58% of science teachers, 62% of mathematics and 92% of English language claimed to be implementing assessment procedures which had a 'high formative element', even if only through the reporting of 'learning needs' and 'next steps' in the pupil's record. However, interviews indicated that while English teachers had some vision of the formative use of assessment, in other subject areas assessment meant end-of-Unit tests and the idea of any kind of assessment as part of a cyclical or interactive process of teaching rather than as an end point was something that only a few secondary teachers had recognised and were struggling to come to terms with. As one mathematics teacher indicated, 'the ethos of the cyclical style keeps coming back to haunt me' (Simpson and Goulder, 1998a).

In the primary schools, 40% of primary teachers indicated that they were now giving more feedback to pupils, and 45% that they had increased the extent to which they used assessment to identify areas where pupils need help. No systematically gathered data was available, however, on the kind of information gathered by teachers as evidence of the nature of difficulties and the subsequent action taken, although there were a few indications that for some teachers the problems identified may have been of a fairly traditional type – 'Are they not listening properly? . . . Am I going too fast? . . . Maybe they've forgotten' (Malcolm and Schlapp, 1997). But there was some evidence from in-service work that there was at least tendency for assessment to be built in throughout the lesson plans and not merely applied at the end.

From a variety of sources it was possible to collate evidence of some imaginative, thoughtful and innovative practices developed by teachers (Simpson, 1997; 2001) but it was clear that these were isolated individual initiatives and were frequently short lived. Formative assessment largely remained at the level of rhetoric for the majority of practitioners. Nevertheless, important advances had been made. Within the Scottish educational system interactions between policy makers, practitioners and researchers take place within a relatively small professional community and while this has its dangers, there are clearly advantages associated with its size and relative stability. From the late 1970s there was a small cadre of professionals within the policy making system who had a clear enough grasp of the importance and educational potential of formative assessment to be committed to promote it, protect it and perpetuate it throughout the complex policy making procedures of the Scottish Office (Simpson and Hayward, 1998b). Initially confined to a small group of individuals, understanding of and commitment to the concept had gradually extended until there was a critical mass of professionals at all levels within the educational system – teachers, teacher educators, researchers, local government officers, inspectors and civil servants – to ensure that even during the period throughout the 1980s and 1990s when the ideology of managerialism and the strategies of summative assessment for accountability were in the ascendant, the formative processes were neither ignored or devalued as they had been in England where little official interest had been evidenced in supporting the development of formative teacher assessment (Whetton, 1997).

Phase 2: Policy, research and practice: learning together

Revitalising political and professional interest
Throughout the 1990s there was a decided lull in both the research undertaken in Scotland and in the sporadic developments undertaken by teachers. Debate and activities continued to be dominated by concerns about National Testing, the outcomes of the national and international monitoring programme and Scotland's position in the international league tables (see Chapter 5). The legacy of political and ideological disputes throughout the 1990s had left the summative systems of assessment within 5–14 in some confusion (see Chapter 2) and any sporadic teacher-initiated formative assessment developments were marginalised and faltering. While many teachers were now very familiar with the superficial vocabulary of 'diagnostic' or 'formative' assessment, the practices of the overwhelming majority of teachers did not match the models associated with significant and informed changes in pedagogy to meet learners' needs. There had been some initial interest in the support materials in the primary sector, but secondary school teachers who could even recall having seen a copy of *Taking a Closer Look* were hard to find. The main problem for those who had retained a commitment to securing the place of formative assessment in both policy and practice remained: how did one establish the integration and productive interaction of policy, research and practice?

Although the HMI review of assessment in 1999 (see Chapter 1) was largely concerned with potential reforms to summative assessment procedures, the perceived importance of formative assessment was clearly stated:

> Whatever changes to the overall assessment system are considered necessary, assessment in the classroom as part of effective teaching and learning will continue to be at the heart of effective assessment . . .This kind of assessment, which involves pupils in decisions about their own learning, is likely to be most effective in raising standards of attainment. (Scottish Executive, 1999, p. 29)

A general professional affirmation of the principles of *5–14 Assessment* (by then 3–14) was reported in the independent scrutiny of the responses to the consultation document (Hayward *et al.*, 2000). But how could these formative principles find secure and practical expression in classrooms? Change in the core dimensions of teaching such as classroom discourse patterns or roles and responsibilities in the teaching–learning relationship is arduous and complex. As the history of formative assessment in Scotland had already shown, the model of using policy to introduce pedagogical change through staff development initiatives based on research appeared to be flawed and had similarly failed in a range of other national and international settings.

Nevertheless, those who believed that formative assessment was a key vehicle for improving learning had to persuade the politicians who were focused on their public commitment to raising standards that developments in this particular area of education would be worth significant resourcing. Was there evidence it would actually bring tangible or measurable learning benefits? And if so, how could teachers be induced to implement formative practices more effectively than they had been in the past?

The impetus to progress came in the form of an accessible publication by Paul Black and his colleagues at King's College, London who had maintained their programme of research on formative assessment throughout the 1990s: *Inside the Black Box* (Black and Wiliam, 1998a). This presented an accessible argument setting out the virtues of formative assessment, starting with the simple question of key import to politicians and educational managers – 'Is there evidence that improving formative assessment raises standards?' And the authors answered it with a persuasively illustrated and unequivocal 'Yes'. This document, and the more substantial academic review on which it was based (Black and Wiliam, 1998b), was used by those within the policy making system who had retained their commitment to the furtherance of formative assessment to stimulate interest at ministerial level and in a series of seminars SEED introduced Dylan Wiliam and the ideas of the King's College researchers to the wider educational community in Scotland. The key questions which then had to be addressed were: What exactly are we encouraging teachers to adopt in their practices? And how can they most effectively be encouraged to do it?

Reconceptualising formative assessment
Generally speaking, whether triggered by the outcomes of a diagnostic test or of teachers' ongoing classroom activities, the processes of investigation and remediation promoted by the earlier models of diagnostic and formative assessment matched fairly well with the standard model of the teacher as the skilled professional who has sole possession of the required specialist knowledge and who determines and controls the transactions within the classroom. Torrance and Prior (2001) noted that the teachers in their study (mainly assessment co-ordinators) who volunteered to work in their action research project from an enthusiasm to develop formative assessment, had a fairly narrow view of what constituted such assessment and the teacher's role within it. It was seen largely as a formal requirement, essentially an additional task or activity to gather information or generate a pupil product to assist the planning of teaching. From the early 1990s however, within research circles, there had been an increasing

acknowledgement of an additional, and potentially more problematical requirement, if formative assessment was to fulfil its full potential – that of a far more informed and proactive participation on the part of the pupils (Sadler, 1989). Added to this was a significant shift in emphasis from a focus on effective teaching to a focus on effective learning. Underlying the currently emerging model is a vision of outcomes beyond mere competence and attainment in subject examinations. In the present period of rapid technological change, school leavers need more than basic knowledgeability as indicators of attainment, it is also essential that they gain the capacity to learn throughout life and to adapt to new environments. They have, therefore, to be motivated and committed to continued learning, to be self-determined, to feel they have the power to promote their own development, and to have confidence that they can succeed and continue to progress. This requires the learner to develop attributes of self-motivation, self-monitoring, self-reflection and self-reliance in learning. In order to promote these characteristics, teachers have been enjoined to give pupils a more active and responsible role in the management of their own learning. However, giving pupils responsibility which is effective and meaningful necessarily involves the sharing of professional knowledge and skills – including full and informed participation in the processes of assessment which are central to the guidance of learning. As Black (1993) noted:

> The development of self-assessment by pupils and students is still in its early stages, but within the framework of formative assessment as an integral part of learning, it seems a natural, almost essential development, as well as a potentially powerful source for the improvement of learning. (p. 82)

And he identified the key characteristics of an effective self-assessment scheme which include: clear, shared criteria; giving students more responsibility for determining their own learning goals; and assessment procedures and recording schemes which are sufficiently clear and economical that students can work them for themselves.

Ideas derived from research, and increasingly made accessible to teachers (Fisher, 1995), also suggest that children are born with much greater potential than hitherto acknowledged and that considerable limitations on school learning outcomes may be set by the standard practices and expectancies of the classroom settings. The implications of these ideas go far beyond the fine tuning of current assessment strategies or the simple replacement of one assessment scheme by another. As the opening quotation of this chapter indicates, the requirements of effective support for learning means that even apparently skilled teachers, as well as their pupils, must adopt novel practices which may be alien to their established repertoire, mainly through a shift of emphasis from thinking and knowing about teaching to thinking and knowing about learning:

Teachers need the confidence that they can make anyone learn as long as they go about it in the right way, confidence that is needed because devotion to formative assessment is risky, taking a great deal of time and energy. In particular, since many pupils may have acquired habits of doing just enough to get by, or have ceased to believe that they can be competent at the subject, the contract between teacher and pupil has to be reformulated. (Black, 1993).

For effective formative assessment it appears necessary that:

- assessment is reconceptualised as a process central to and shared within the regular teacher and learner interaction rather than as a procedure at the end of instruction directed judgementally towards the pupil, or used to inform the teacher alone;
- there are changes in the teachers' conceptions of pupils' abilities and potential leading to the adoption of the view that all pupils can learn more effectively given the appropriate context, information, and support;
- there is an articulation of the learning goals considered appropriate for pupils in general and for individuals when engaging in specific classroom activities which are devised to help pupils meet these goals (rather than to cover certain topics);

and finally,

- there is a change from pupils being passive recipients of educational instruction and measurement, to being knowledgeable and proactive in the pursuance of successful learning strategies.

The term 'formative assessment' is therefore defined by Black and Wiliam (1998a) as 'encompassing all those activities undertaken by teachers, and by their students in assessing themselves, which provide information to be used as feedback to modify the teaching and learning activities in which they are engaged' (p. 2). Although teachers' activities can be identified which exemplify formative principles in action, these principles could be exemplified through a wide range of different practices as appropriate for different contexts with respect to subjects, pupils and teachers. Many studies seemed to indicate that teachers themselves were best placed to design their own formative activities, but needed some framework from research to give guidance on what would constitute the type and quality of interactions which would bring the desired learning gains. For example, giving feedback to pupils is a central formative activity, but all teachers could confidently claim that they already did this. What was so special or different about the kind of feedback that could truly be described as comprising effective formative assessment?

In a follow-up publication, *Working Inside the Black Box*, Black and his colleagues (2002) identified a small number of focal points for thinking about development in classrooms and these formed the research input of the AifL programme of development *Support for Professional Practice in Formative Assessment* (L&T Scotland, 2003) which was launched in May 2002:

- *The importance of questions:* particularly those designed to prompt pupil engagement, discussion and thought rather than to check correct acquisition of specific information. The effective use of wait time (Rowe, 1974) was re-emphasised.
- *The importance of useful feedback* on pupils' work: the research findings presented to teachers included the startling evidence that if marks were not given for work, just useful pointers to making further progress, pupils engaged more productively in improving their work.
- *Peer- and self-assessment:* pupils could only achieve goals if they understood what they were trying to attain and how to attain it. Giving pupils appropriate support to develop their skills in self- and peer-assessment was a key to securing motivated learners working increasingly at a meta-cognitive level to manage and control their own learning.

Reconceptualising the policy implementation process

While policymakers and reformers at all levels of the system are crucial if reforms are to be enacted locally, teachers are the key agents when it comes to changing classroom practice: they are the final policy brokers. (Spillane, 1999, p. 144)

Clearly, the introduction of this even more challenging concept of formative assessment requires significant changes to take place in the thinking and practices of many teachers, and a redefining of their roles and of the power relationships between them and their pupils. Indeed, Black refers to formative assessment as 'a Trojan Horse' with respect to innovation in pedagogy (Black, 2001, p. 76). In what contexts, and with what incentives, models and support could Scottish teachers be assisted to engage more successfully than previously in ambitious development activities of this type? Two things were required: a fresh impetus to rekindle and sustain enthusiasm for development, and a process of development that would centrally involve teachers in the design of innovative practice. However, both of these required an even more problematic shift of trust and power – from the policy makers to the teachers. The fact that the risk of this devolution of responsibility was taken by the politicians was no doubt in some measure due to the fact that the First Minister had himself been a teacher. The call to 'trust the teachers' fell on listening ears.

Nevertheless, a sound case based on evidence had to be made. The programme of development which was strategically planned and initiated was based not only on research which advocated formative assessment as a potentially powerful means of raising standards through the improvement in those classroom practices which impinged on learning, but also on research which addressed the shortcomings of previous policy implementation strategies and how to improve these (Hayward *et al.*, 2004; Hayward and Hedge, 2005; Hutchinson and Hayward, 2005). The work of Guile was noted, in which the context of work is presented as the location in which situated knowledge production is based, with the intellect and creativity of the employees as the resources of production (Guile, 2003). The knowledge is powerful because it is generated and situated in the social context where it is to be usefully applied. This contrasts with the typical policy implementation model based on learning as the acquisition of pre-existing knowledge generated outside classrooms (from research), with staff development as the vehicle for the constant updating of skills and knowledge (through dissemination documents and cascade events). This form of teaching (by policy makers and researchers) and learning (by teachers) replicates the transmission model typically applied by teachers to pupils, and has the same fairly low level of effectiveness. The knowledge acquired is 'inert' and superficially understood and applied. A second major influence came from the extended work by Black and Wiliam in the King's–Medway–Oxfordshire Project. Although information from research was introduced, teachers involved in the project had not been told what to do, but were invited to experiment, explore, develop and evaluate approaches to formative assessment in their classrooms. The third main research influence came from the work on transformational learning, in particular that of Senge and Sharmer (2001) and their analysis of collaborative action research approaches.

This input led to a programme based on the sound educational principle that learning should begin where all those involved are starting from: professionally, individually, collectively, emotionally and politically. 'Learning for teachers, researchers and policy makers in this project is not simply about the acquisition of knowledge and skills but has to involve learning how to transform communities of practice' (Hayward *et al.*, 2004, p. 400). Rather than prompts and support in the form of information and exemplification as in previous policy initiatives, the impetus for development took the form of allocated time and money – resources which teachers could deploy as they wished on their development work. A large scale programme of meetings was organised which, in the initial stages, had input from researchers and enthusiastic teachers from the Black and Wiliam project who had 'walked this way before', but which also, and more importantly, had presentations from Scottish teachers who were themselves engaged in different AifL projects. Regular opportunities were created for the coming together of teachers for sharing and discussion of their activities, ideas and successes.

The network of involvement extended to schools in every Authority, and support was offered through development officers from L&T

Scotland, and Local Authority assessment co-ordinators, charged with the responsibility of developing mechanisms for the extension of activities from their project schools throughout their area. These resources and activities created the scaffolding and social context within which teachers could comfortably experiment and learn through the development of innovations in their own practice. In an analysis of teachers as learners Spillane, (1999) identified the 'zones of enactment' – that zone in which reform initiatives are encountered by the world of practice, in which teachers notice, construe, reconstruct and operationalise the ideas advocated by research and policy. By providing the conditions to optimise the supportive features in this zone the policy makers initiated a nationwide experiment in the application of constructivist, collaborative, work-based learning to the teaching profession.

As Hayward *et al.* (2004) note, not all schools and teachers have been wholly successful in their engagement, but an analysis of the contributing factors to the range of successful and unsuccessful outcomes gives reason to believe the seeds of development were indeed sown in well prepared fertile ground. From Hayward's research and from subsequent data collected, two common findings emerge: the high level of engagement, confidence and enthusiasm of the teachers in the development, and their reports of increased levels of pupils' engagement in class work and their pupils' increased confidence and enthusiasm for the learning strategies introduced. Many expressed surprise at how insightful and articulate pupils could be about their own learning.

With respect to the further development of pupils as confident, informed and independent learners, an ultimately critical element in the plan for a coherent assessment system is the ambitious concept of 'personal learning planning' which is located in the formative quadrant of the overall assessment scheme (see Chapter 1). Although initially construed by some teachers in the development projects as merely the requirement for a detailed record of attainment and a forward plan for further achievements, it was originally conceived, more creatively and ambitiously, as an ongoing conversation between the pupil, the teachers and the parents, with the pupil as the principal custodian of any record of the process. Its fundamental aim is to provide a context for talking about learning and to devolve ownership of the learning to the learner by engaging pupils in the planning, management and monitoring of their own learning, developing their capacity to understand what is to be learned, how and why, and increasingly to understand their learning strengths and weaknesses and to take responsibility for their own development – *Assessment as Learning* (L&T Scotland, 2003). Whether this more difficult and complex aspect of assessment can be developed as innovatively as it potentially could be will depend on the ability of teachers themselves to be effective learners, to engage with and understand the new concepts and purposes involved, and to avoid the default position of seeing the requirement as the compilation of unhelpful and detailed paper records with few merits and significant workload implications. Isolated individual practitioners have undertaken such innovative developments in the past (Simpson, 2001), the more ambitious aim of this current policy is to extend understanding and practice throughout the educational system.

CHAPTER 7

ASSESSMENT FOR THE TWENTY-FIRST CENTURY

Our mistake, with hindsight, has been to believe that learning can be assessed accurately and reliably. The shift that is taking place in assessment can be seen as part of a shift in our world view. (Gipps, 1996, p. 12)

As the accounts in this book have illustrated, the assessment practices currently applied in Scottish schools and the revisions planned for the immediate future can be viewed as socio-political in origins and ultimately shaped in their educational detail by historical understanding of learning and teaching, the stability of long established professional practices and by compromises negotiated between powerful factions with conflicting political, social and professional interests. The same is likely to be true of assessment systems in most other countries. But as Gipps (1996) indicates, our understanding of learning has changed and for the twenty-first century, there are quite new and challenging perspectives on the world.

The established view of assessment and the curriculum

Although experienced professionals in education perceive that much has changed over their working life, it could be argued that very little has fundamentally changed concerning the underlying philosophy and central concepts which have informed and shaped the assessment systems of most educational services. Assessment is still largely regarded by teachers – and the general public – as being separate from and external to the teaching and learning process and context, and as requiring systems developed by technicians or measurement experts to judge accurately and reliably the learning outcomes with respect to pupils' efficiency in learning predetermined knowledge or skills, and the teachers' efficiency in imparting these. Pupil performance or knowledge and understanding are judged with little regard to the social context in which these have been generated, and the final judgements, typically made by means of a formal assessment on a specific day, focus on the individual pupil.

This model, and its rationale and values are now deeply embedded in our national psyche, and however dated with respect to current learning theory, these kinds of assessment devices align well with the current models of curriculum and pedagogy and valued school learning outcomes in Scottish schools. But because these complementary educational components and the associated certification examination systems legitimise the fairly static subject knowledge and competencies of teachers in secondary school subjects they seriously limit innovation in curriculum and pedagogy. Many recent technologically based innovations – the downloading of tests, the setting of tests for different ability levels, provision of instant feedback on learners' wrong answers, computerised marking – all assist the hard pressed teacher / assessor to run the current systems more effectively, but also perpetuate them with little real challenge or change.

There are growing tensions between eliciting the pupils' best performance, or their demonstration of the co-ordination of diverse skills and knowledge in creative, complex or authentic contexts, and standardisation for reliability through external examinations. In the minds of many practitioners and educational managers, the latter feature is linked to scientific accuracy, fairness for the learner, certainty and security for the teacher, and defensibility with respect to standards in the wider public forum. But this is antithetical to aspirations to organise the curriculum and assessment so that more young people are encouraged to stay on longer within the formal educational system, to be motivated and equipped to keep coming back to education throughout their lives and to develop the skills and dispositions necessary for the citizens of an effective and thriving modern economy and culture. Learning in the typical school of the twentieth century is increasingly seen as an inadequate preparation for life in the twenty-first century.

A view of curriculum and assessment for the twenty-first century

> Outside of school the media grab for attention with a stream of technicolour images featuring global heroes and soundbites. Inside the school the standard fare comprises monochrome worksheets and unheroic talking heads. The two worlds are at odds. If the school is perceived as not only imposed and inflexible but also outmoded and dull then its ability to persuade modern youth to swallow their curriculum medicine will be limited. (Conlon, 2000, p. 112)

The narrowly focused, school-subject demarcated, monochrome curriculum is indeed outdated, given the present pace of societal change and readily accessible mass communication systems and knowledge sources. The content of many school subjects relates less and less to the fields of interest in areas of public concern and importance, such as financial management, cloning or global warming, or to the disciplines that have emerged in universities. Where the misalignment with the external world is greatest, for example in the sciences, the level of pupil engagement, and consequently their attainment is weakest (HMIE, 2005; TESS, 2005). And in the future, the basis of national prosperity will depend increasingly not on school knowledge reproduction, or even on regular updating, but on the creation and use of knowledge for problem solving in open-ended, less predictable contexts than at present. Complex, dynamic forms of knowledge characteristically produced in action, through experience and in social environments will be significant. The pedagogy of the twenty-first century must anticipate this new social context and requirements, and the characteristics of current paradigms of teaching and learning must change accordingly.

At present, de-contextualised 'school work' dominates pupil learning, comprising artificial problems, tasks or projects, with an overall focus on the transmission of well-established knowledge from the teacher who is the main source of information. Linear progression in the acquisition of closed, pre-specified knowledge and skills proceeds by learning, practicing and application. Learning groups comprise 'homogeneous' groupings of learners, put together through date of birth, or setting on the basis of unreliable measures of attainment in narrow areas of compartmentalised and fragmented subject areas. Both learning and assessment are conceived as solitary, individual efforts with large degrees of social competitiveness.

In contrast, emerging paradigms of teaching and learning have successfully incorporated social-constructivist based strategies. The multiple sources of expertise and information now available are used to enable authentic tasks to be posed, contextualised in meaningful situations, linked to purposeful products, and to incorporate cross-discipline information, e.g. a plan of possible effects of global warming on aspects of the local area. Many skills are learned in the process of purposeful application, and the activities enable the development of complex, richly linked conceptual structures supported by social interactions in heterogeneous groupings of learners who can use and display their diverse talents to contribute to processes of knowledge generation in the group (Simpson, 2000).

The diverse forms of assessment necessary to align with these new forms of curriculum and pedagogy take a variety of forms – but are typically set in the context of the learning, within complex tasks and cover a range of 'performance-based assessment' or 'authentic assessment' including portfolios, mini-investigations, etc. (for examples see Mueller, 2004). Such assessments mirror the real world and require students to integrate purposeful assimilation and use of knowledge through diverse strategies, and educators to use a more holistic and flexible approach when determining criteria for and scores from the assessment. Portfolio assessment is perhaps the most common form of authentic assessment and in its broadest sense is a purposeful collection of the individual's work.

For much of the curriculum of the future, such as that implied by *A Curriculum for Excellence* (Scottish Executive, 2004a), a well constructed authentic task should have higher validity than an objective multiple choice, essay or constructed response test, since the attributes which it assesses are more nearly isomorphic with the constructs of interest – ability to think, reason, integrate skills, apply sound judgement and creativity to key aspects of the task. Such assessments do not, of course, serve every function, and are intended to complement rather than replace the teachers' repertoire of existing assessment tools which measure uptake and recall of information. However, teachers need to become more confident in the conception, writing and application of such tasks and understand how secure criteria can be set to assess the performance of pupils. Within some educational systems in which there are no final external examinations, internal assessment by teachers, supported by levels of school, local and state-wide moderation mechanisms is well established and clearly lends itself to the accommodation of innovative development in curriculum and assessment in ways that the external examination systems of Scotland do not (Sebba and Maxwell, 2004).

Clearly an appropriate bridge between formative assessment activities of teacher–leaner interaction in classrooms and the formal external national monitoring of the SSA and international surveys could be created by moderated, but internally applied, summative assessments of pupils at transition and exit points. One might speculate that the current emphasis by SEED on developing teachers' assessment skills through moderation and 'sharing of standards' and the presence of presenters from Queensland at several recent SEED assessment seminars is an indication that this possibility for the future is in the minds of the policy makers. However, if developed and established, these emerging paradigms of curriculum, pedagogy and assessment would begin to introduce new teaching and learning relationships into highly conservative and traditional organisations. What policy and practice contexts would be conducive to such change in the future?

The policy and practice contexts for change in Scotland

As Chapters 2 to 4 have illustrated, the present assessment systems have largely been derived from centrally initiated, 'top-down' developments, frequently in the context of a lack of consensus emerging following open consultation and debate. Nevertheless, educational policymaking generally in Scotland has eschewed the quasi-market system of England, with its strongly centrally controlled, managerialist approaches applied in an ethos of general mistrust of the teachers. Major disagreements in Scotland have focussed primarily on resourcing and workload rather than on educational or ideological principles. Recently there have been clear indicators of the Scottish government's commitment to generating productive working relationships with the teaching profession, to promoting their autonomous professional development and to devolving to schools decisions concerning the curriculum and its management which were formerly taken centrally. These initiatives include the McCrone Agreement (Scottish Executive, 2001a), the Chartered Teacher Professional Development Programme (Scottish Executive, 2002b), the funding allocated to a wide range of school-initiated developments such as the FLaT programme (L&T Scotland, 2002) and Curriculum Flexibility, (L&T Scotland, 2001) and finally the AifL programme (see Chapter 6).

The responses of the teaching profession to these policy overtures have not been overwhelmingly positive. It seems that in the hierarchical world of the teaching culture, decisions should only be made by those paid as managers to do so.

> Indeed, so suspicious are the teacher unions of the possibility that Chartered Teachers might be used to undertake management tasks within schools, that at the time of writing no programmes in leadership for Chartered Teachers, teachers who are likely to be leading experts in teaching and learning in their schools, are likely to be developed. (O'Brien *et al.*, 2003, p. 55)

Perhaps their negative attitudes are justifiably due to memories of past impositions and stand offs but many have inappropriately adopted the rhetoric of derision and mistrust between government and teaching profession from south of the border, despite the quite different policy context of the past twenty years and the fact that their pay and conditions of service are now extremely enhanced in comparison with those other professionals also charged with the care and education of young people – the early educators, childcare staff and social workers.

The innovative and successful aspects of educational initiatives such as the 5–14 curriculum guidelines and ICT adoption (Simpson and Payne, 2004) have worked incomparably better in primary schools, where staff groups evidence the strategies and skills of learning communities, than in secondary schools where the capacity of the fiefdoms of the subject departments to resist change is monumental. It is of some concern that the characteristic approach of teachers to their own learning is a curious one for professionals engaged in the business of education. Studies indicate they have a low engagement with other educators from outside their small, immediate professional circle and they typically ignore outside sources of information such as the professional and research literature: 'Books like that (Eraut, Pollard) were for management candidates, not classroom teachers like me' (*Scottish Education Journal*, 2004). They learn new pedagogical routines primarily by word of mouth and hands on, trial-and-error learning, and the autonomy of the individual teacher to pursue their own classroom agenda, however dated, leads to huge variations in pupils' daily learning experiences (Boyd and Simpson, 2000;

Simpson *et al.*, 2005). This closed professional culture is not unique to Scotland. In a US study, 'Lack of external information coalesced with self–interest in the status quo, and was reinforced by selective attention to those to those elements in their value system that stressed the continuation of current practice' (Weiss, 1995, p. 587).

There will be many learning difficulties to be overcome in the schools of Scotland in the next few years of the twenty-first century as they struggle to modernise.

ASSESSMENT IN SCOTTISH SCHOOLS

Assessment level or award	Additional information	Means of assessment
Early Years	Individual profiles	Observational recordings
Baseline/Transition Assessment	Often done at start of P1, but timing can vary depending on the type of system used by the Local Authority	Internally-recorded, individual, competency-based assessments.
5–14 National Assessment (Formerly National Tests)	Primary P1–P7 and Secondary S1–S2 Aspects of English language and mathematics only	National Assessment Bank Materials provided electronically by SQA; internally assessed – fixed marking criteria.
SCE Standard Grade) (14–16 year age group)	(Foundation (grades 5–6) General (grades 3–4) Credit (grades 1–2)	Some elements marked internally (moderated by SQA) External papers marked by SQA
National Qualifications **Access 1** (SCQF level 1)	Supported level units Independent level units Individualised performance criteria (usually drawn from Access 2 Units, 'elaborated 5-14' and 'achievement mapping schemes')	Internal (moderated by SQA)
Access 2 (SCQF level 2)	Skillstart (Access 2) Range of curricular models	Internal (moderated by SQA)
Access 3 (SCQF level 3) **(Standard Grade: Foundation)**	National link with SCOTVEC 1 Modules Skillstart (Access 3) benchmarked to Foundation level	Internal (moderated by SQA)

Intermediate 1 (SCQF level 4) **(Standard Grade: General)**	GSVQ 1 Benchmarked to General level	Individual units internally assessed as pass/fail (some are based on old National Certificate Awards) All include Core Skills
Intermediate 2 (SCQF level 5) **(Standard Grade: Credit)**	GSVQ 2. Benchmarked to Credit level	Profile to some extent: (communication, numeracy, information technology, problem-solving, working
Higher (SCQF level 6)	GSVQ 3	with others) Course external exams or Project Based NCs
Advanced Higher (SCQF level 7)	A Level (grades A–C)	(SQA National Qualifications) A–C pass grades.
SGA (Scottish Group Awards) General awards (available Access 2 through to Advanced Higher) Also named awards at Intermediate 2 and Higher		Combinations of clusters or courses, sometimes incorporating free-standing units can be built up into SGAs

KEY EVENTS IN POLICY WHICH INFLUENCED ASSESSMENT

Comprehensivisation of the secondary school system	*1960s*
Introduction of the O-Grade into secondary schools	*1962*
Raising of the school leaving age from 15 to 16	*1972*
Publication of the Munn Report: *The Structure of the Curriculum in the Third and Fourth Years of Secondary Education in Scotland*; and the Dunning Report: *Assessment for All – Report of the Committee to Review Assessment in the Third and Fourth Years of Secondary Education in Scotland.*	*1977*
Development and introduction of the Standard Grade curriculum and the examination structures	*1980s*
Publication of *16–18 in Scotland: An Action Plan*	*1983*
Teachers' industrial action for improved pay and conditions started	*1984*
Publication of the CCC report: *Education 10–14 in Scotland*	*1986*
Michael Forsyth became Education Minister Salaries and conditions of service agreement for teachers published as Circular SE/40 ending two-year dispute	*1987*
Publication of *Curriculum and Assessment in Scotland: a Policy for the 1990s* introducing a rationale for the 5–14 initiatives	*1987*
School Boards established	*1988*
Ian Lang became Education Minister	*1989*

Ian Lang became Scottish Secretary with Michael Forsyth again becoming Education Minister	*1990*
Publication of the Draft Guidelines on National Assessment and Testing	*1990*
Formation of the Parents' Coalition	*1991*
Lord James Douglas-Hamilton became Education Minister	*1992*
Howie Report recommended end to post-16 divide between academic and vocational qualifications	*1992*
Publication of *Higher Still: Opportunity for All*	*1994*
Donald Dewar became Scottish Secretary with Brian Wilson, and later Helen Liddell as Education Minister	*1997*
Publication of the HMI *Review of Assessment in pre-school and 5–14*	*1999*
The Scottish Parliament opened with Donald Dewar as First Minister and Sam Galbraith as Minister for Children and Education	*1999*
McCrone Report on teachers' pay and conditions published. The Agreement which set out implementation details came one year later.	*2000*
Higher Still reforms put into place Scottish Qualifications Authority failed to send correct results to all candidates	*2000*
Standards in Scottish Schools Act	*2000*
Publication of outcomes of consultation on assessment and testing (Glasgow University)	*December 2000*
Debate in the Scottish Parliament on *Effective Assessment for Scotland's Schools*	*September 2001*
An Action Group is established to oversee a programme of reform, *Assessment is for Learning*	*November 2001*
National Debate launched on purposes of school education	*April 2002*
Educating for Excellence: The Governments response to the National Debate	*January 2003*
Consultation on Partnership Agreements on assessment	*August 2003*

The Curriculum Review Group convened	*November 2003*
Publication of *A Curriculum for Excellence* (SEED)	*November 2004*
Publication of *Assessment Testing and Reporting 3–14: Our response* (SEED)	*November 2004*
Publication of *Outcomes of Partnership Agreement Consultations* (Strathclyde University)	*November 2004*
A Curriculum for Excellence: Ministerial Response	*November 2004*

BIBLIOGRAPHY

Adams, R. J. (2003) 'Response to "Caution on OECD's recent educational survey (PISA)" ', *Oxford Review of Education*, Vol. 29, No. 3, pp. 377–89. Available from URL: www.oecd.org/dataoecd/29/50/33680709.pdf (accessed 22 June 2005)

Arnold, B. Wilson, J. and MacKenzie, W. (1984) *Foundation Item Banking Science* (FIBS), Aberdeen: Aberdeen College of Education

Askew, M., Brown, M., Rhodes, V., Wiliams, D. and Johnson, D. (1997) *Effective Teachers of Numeracy in the Primary School*, London: King's College School of Education

Assessment of Achievement Programme (AAP) (1993) *Mathematics Feedback 2*, Edinburgh: SOED

Assessment of Achievement Programme (1995) *Science Feedback 2*, Edinburgh: SOED

Black, H. D. (1983) 'Introducing diagnostic assessment', *Programmed Learning and Educational Technology*, Vol. 20, No. 1, pp. 58–63

Black, H. D. and Dockrell, W. B. (1984) *Criterion Referenced Assessment in the Classroom*, Edinburgh: SCRE

Black, P. (1993) 'Formative and summative assessment by teachers', *Studies in Science Education*, Vol. 21, pp. 49–97

Black, P. (2001) 'Dreams, strategies and systems: portraits of assessment past, present and future', *Assessment in Education*, Vol. 8, No. 1, pp. 66–85

Black, P. and Wiliam, D. (1998a) *Inside the Black Box*, London: Kings College, London University. Available from URL: www.ltscotland.org.uk/assess/projects_project_1.asp (accessed 1 June 2005)

Black, P. J. and Wiliam, D. (1998b) 'Assessment and classroom learning', *Assessment in Education*, Vol. 5, No. 1, pp. 7–74

Black, P., Harrison, C., Lee, C., Marshall, B. and Wiliam, D. (2002) *Working Inside the Black Box: Assessment for Learning in the Classroom*, Slough: National Foundation for Educational Research–Nelson

Boyd, B. (1994) 'The management of curriculum development: the 5–14 programme', in W. Humes and M. L. Mackenzie (eds) *The Management of Educational Policy*, Harlow: Longman, pp. 17–30

Boyd, B. and Simpson, M. (2000) *Developing a Framework for Effective Learning and Teaching in S1 and S2*, Forfar: Angus Council

Boyd, B. and Simpson, M. (2003) 'Primary/secondary liaison', in Bryce and Humes (eds) (2003), pp. 362–6

Briggs, S. (1992) 'Eurodunce?' *Scotland on Sunday*, 13 December

Brown, S. (1980) *What Do They Know? A Review of Criterion-Referenced Assessment*, Edinburgh: HMSO

Brown, S. (1990) 'The National Curriculum and testing: enlightened or imported?' *Scottish Educational Review*, Vol. 22, No. 2, pp. 68–77

Brown, S. and Munn, P. (1985) *The Changing Face of Education 14–16: Curriculum and Assessment*, Windsor: National Foundation for Educational Research–Nelson

Bryce, T. G. K. (1993) 'Constructivism, knowledge and national science targets', *Scottish Educational Review*, Vol. 25, No. 2, pp. 87–96

Bryce, T. G. K. (2003) 'Could do Better?', in Bryce and Humes (eds) (2003), pp. 709–20

Bryce, T. G. K. and Humes, W. (1999) *Scottish Education*, (1st edn), Edinburgh: Edinburgh University Press

Bryce, T. G. K. and Humes, W. (2003) *Scottish Education*, (2nd edn): Post-Devolution, Edinburgh: Edinburgh University Press

Condie, R., Robertson, I. and Napuk, A. (2003) 'The Assessment of Achievement Programme', in Bryce and Humes (eds) (2003), pp. 766–76

Conlon, T. (2000) 'Visions of change: information technology, education and postmodernism', *British Journal of Educational Technology*, Vol. 31, No. 2, pp. 109–16

Consultative Committee on the Curriculum (1986) *Education 10–14 in Scotland*, Dundee: CCC

Courier (1994) 'Chances of National Tests boycott look to be fading', 16 September

Croxford, L. (1997) 'Participation in science subjects: the effects of the Scottish Curriculum Framework', *Research Papers in Education*, Vol. 12, No. 1, pp. 69–89

Croxford, L., Howieson, C., and Raffe, D. (1991) 'National Certificate modules in the S5 curriculum', *Scottish Educational Review*, Vol. 23, No. 2, pp. 78–92

Croxford, L., Tinklin, T., Frame, B. and Ducklin, A. (2003) 'Gender and pupil performance: where do the problems lie?', *Scottish Educational Review*, Vol. 35, No. 2, pp. 135–47

Darling, J. (2003) 'Scottish primary education: philosophy and practice', in Bryce and Humes (eds) (2003), pp. 27–36

Daugherty, R. (1995) *National Curriculum Assessment: A Review of Policy 1987–1994*, London: Falmer Press

De Luca, C. (2003) 'SQA findings on Scottish achievements', in Bryce and Humes (eds) (2003), pp. 777–94

Delandshere, G. (2002) 'Assessment as enquiry', *Teachers College Record*, Vol. 104, No. 7, pp. 1461–84

Department for Education and Skills (2005) *14–19 Education and Skills* (Tomlinson Report), Cm6476, London: The Stationery Office

Drever, E. (1985) 'Mastery learning in context', in Brown and Munn (eds) (1985), pp. 58–68

Educational Institute of Scotland (1991) *The National Test: Guidelines for School Representatives and Members*, Edinburgh: EIS, February

Eleftheriou, M. (1985) 'School-based developments in foundation English', in Brown and Munn (eds) (1985), pp. 10–20

Fisher, R. (1995) *Teaching Children to Learn*, Cheltenham: Stanley Thornes

Forsyth, M. et al. (1986) *Save Our Schools*, London: Conservative Political Centre

Gillespie, J. (1997) *National Testing – The Inside Story*, Edinburgh: private publication

Gilmore A. (2005) *The Impact of PIRLS (2001) and TIMSS (2003) In Low and Middle-Income Countries*. Available from URL: www.iea.nl/iea/hq/ (accessed 22 June 2005)

Gipps, C. (1996) *Assessment for the Millennium: Form, Function and Feedback*, Inaugural Lecture, London: Institute of Education

Goldstein H. (1996) 'International comparisons of student achievement', in A. Little and A. Wolf (eds) *Assessment in Transition*, New York: Pergamon, pp. 58–87

Goldstein H. (2004) 'International comparative assessment: how far have we really come?' *Assessment in Education*, Vol. 11, No. 2, pp. 227–34

Guile, D. (2003) 'From "credentialism" to the "Practice of Learning": reconceptualising learning for the knowledge economy', *Policy Futures in Education*, Vol. 1, No. 1, pp. 83–105

Harlen, W. (1996) *Four Years of Change in Education 5–14*, Edinburgh: SCRE

Harlen, W. (1997) 'Cause of an unpleasant shiver', *Times Educational Supplement Scotland*, 3 January

Hartley, D. (2003) 'Education and the Scottish economy', in Bryce and Humes (eds) (2003), pp. 282–92

Hayward L. and Hall, J. (1995) *Taking a Closer Look at Reading – Diagnostic Procedures*, Edinburgh: Scottish Council for Research in Education

Hayward, L. and Hedge, N. (2005) 'Travelling towards change in assessment: policy, practice and research in education', *Assessment in Education*, Vol. 12, No. 1, pp. 55–75

Hayward, L., Kane, J. and Kogan, N. (2000) *Improving Assessment in Scotland: Report on the Consultation*, Glasgow: University of Glasgow

Hayward L., Priestley, M. and Young, M. (2004) 'Ruffling the calm of the ocean floor: merging practice, policy and research in assessment in Scotland', *Oxford Review of Education*, Vol. 30, No. 3, pp. 397–415

Her Majesty's Inspectors (1997) *Improving Mathematics Education 5–14*, Edinburgh: SOEID

Hirst, P. (1969) 'The logic of the curriculum', *Journal of Curriculum Studies*, Vol. 1, No. 2, pp. 142–58

HM Inspectorate of Education (2005) *Improving Achievement in Science in Primary and Secondary Schools*, Edinburgh: HMIE. Available from URL: www.hmie.gov.uk/documents/publication/iais.pdf (accessed 27 June 2005)

HM Inspectorate of Education (HMIE) (2002) *How Good is Our School? Self-Evaluation Using Quality Indicators*, Edinburgh: HMIE. Available from URL: www.hmie.gov.uk/documents/publication/ HGIOS.pdf (accessed 29 June 2005)

Howieson, C. and Closs, A. (2005) *The Inclusion of Students with Learning Difficulties within Scotland's Unified Curriculuar System: A Successful Example of Policy Implementation?* Working Paper 10, Centre for Educational Sociology, University of Edinburgh

Howieson, C., Raffe, D. and Tinklin, T. (2004) 'The use of New National Qualifications in S3 and S4 in 2002–3', *Scottish Educational Review*, Vol. 36, No. 2, pp. 177–90

Humes, W. (1986) *The Leadership Class in Scottish Education*, Edinburgh: John Donald

Humes, W. (1995) 'The significance of Michael Forsyth in Scottish education', *Scottish Affairs*, Vol. 11, pp. 112–30

Humes W. and Bryce T. (2000) 'Scholarship, research and the evidential basis of policy development in education', paper presented at European Conference of Educational Research, Edinburgh

Hutchinson, C. and Hayward, L. (2005) 'The journey so far: assessment for learning in Scotland', *The Curriculum Journal*, Vol. 16, No. 2, pp. 225–48

Kirk, G. and Glaister, R. (1994) *5–14: Scotland's National Curriculum*, Edinburgh: Scottish Academic Press

Learning and Teaching Scotland (2001) *The Curriculum Flexibility Initiatives*. Available from URL: www.ltscotland.org.uk/curriculum-flexibility/ (accessed 26 June 2005)

Learning and Teaching Scotland (2002) *The Future Learning and Teaching Programme* (FlaT). Information available from URL: www.flatprojects.org.uk/index.asp (accessed 25 June 2005)

Learning and Teaching Scotland (2003) *About the Assessment is for Learning Programme*. Available from URL: www.ltscotland.org.uk/ assess/about/index.asp (accessed 26 June 2005)

Learning and Teaching Scotland (2004) *Guide to the National Qualifications*. Available from URL: www.ltscotland.org.uk/nq/

files/guidetonqs.pdf (accessed 26 June 2005)
Learning and Teaching Scotland (2005) *The 5–14 Curriculum Guidelines*. Available from URL: www.ltscotland.org.uk/5to14/guidelines/ (accessed 26 June 2005)
Long, H. (1999) 'The Scottish Examination Board', in Bryce and Humes (eds) (2003), pp. 677–87
MacBeath, J. (2003) 'School effectiveness, improvement and self-evaluation', in Bryce and Humes (eds) (2003), pp. 804–13
MacBride, G. (1998) 'Can Higher Still work?', *Scottish Educational Journal*, Vol. 82, No. 2, Edinburgh: Educational Institute of Scotland, p. 6
Maclennan, E. (2004) *Assessment, Testing and Reporting 3–14 – Consultation on Partnership Commitments*. Available from URL: www.scotland.gov.uk/consultations/education/atrcpc-02.asp (accessed 26 June 2005)
McPherson, A. (1989) 'Twists in the numbers game', *Times Educational Supplement Scotland*, 21 April
McPherson, A. (1992a) 'The Howie Committee on post-compulsory schooling', *Scottish Government Yearbook*, Edinburgh: Unit for the Study of Government in Scotland, pp. 114–30
McPherson, A. (1992b) 'Schooling', in Dickson, A. and Treble, J. H. (eds) *People and Society in Scotland*, Vol. III, 1914–1990, Edinburgh: John Donald, pp. 80–107
McPherson, A. (1992c) 'Critical reflections on the Howie Report', in *Critical Reflections on Curriculum Policy*, the SCRE Fellowship Lectures, Edinburgh: Scottish Council for Research in Education, pp. 29–52
Malcolm, H. and Schlapp, U. (1997) *5–14 in Primary Schools: A Continuing Challenge*, Edinburgh: SCRE
Massey, A. Green, S., Dexter, T. and Hamnet, L. (2003) *Comparability of National Tests over Time: Key Stage Test Standards between 1996 and 2001*, Cambridge: University of Cambridge Local Examinations Syndicate. Available from URL: www.nfer.ac.uk/latest-news/ontheweb/pdfs/jan04.pdf (accessed 25 June 2005)
Mitchell, F. (1991) 'Responding to the Framework for National Testing in 1991', *Professional Teacher* (Scottish Supplement)' Summer, pp. 1–2
Mueller, J. (2004) The Authentic Assessment Toolbox. Available from URL: jonathan.mueller.faculty.noctrl.edu/toolbox/whatisit.htm#authentic (accessed 26 June 2005)
Munro, L. (2003) 'National Testing and National Assessments', in Bryce and Humes (eds) (2003), 746–55
Munro, L. and Kimber, P. (1999) 'National Testing', in Bryce and Humes (eds) (2003), pp. 713–21
Murphy, P. (1990) 'National Curriculum Assessment: has anything been learned from the experiences of the APU?', *The Curriculum Journal*,

Vol. 1, No. 2, pp. 185–97

National Center for Educational Statistics (NCES) (2003) *Comparative Indicators of Education in the United States and other G8 Countries: 2002*. Available from URL: nces.ed.gov/pubsearch/pubsinfo.asp? pubid=2005021 (accessed 22 June 2005)

NPACI (1998) 'Poor TIMSS results prompt NSB reaction for core math/science skills'. Available from URL: www.npaci.edu/online/v2. 16/nsb_timss.html (accessed 22 June 2005)

O'Brien, J., Murphy, D. and Draper, J. (2003) *School Leadership*, Policy and Practice in Education 9, Edinburgh: Dunedin Academic Press

OECD (2003) *Programme for International Student Assessment: The PISA 2003 Assessment Framework*. Available from URL: hub.mspnet. org/index.cfm/9445 (accessed 30 June 2005)

Osborn, M., Broadfoot, P., McNess, E., Planel, C., Ravn, B., and Triggs, P. (2003) *A World of Difference? Comparing Learners across Europe*, Maidenhead: Open University Press

Parents' Coalition (1991) *Information Sheet: What Can Parents Do?* Aberdeen: Parents' Coalition

Paterson, L. (2000a) *Education and the Scottish Parliament*, Policy and Practice in Education 1, Edinburgh: Dunedin Academic Press

Paterson, L. (2000b) *Crisis in the Classroom: The Exam Debacle and the Way Ahead for Scottish Education*, Edinburgh: Mainstream Publishing

Payne, F., Gooday, M. and Simpson, M. (2004) *Evaluation of the Moray Council/ Keith Grammar School Standard Grade in S2/3*, Edinburgh University. Available from URL: www.flatprojects.org.uk/index.asp (accessed 30 June 2005)

Pickard, W. and Dobie, J. (2003). *The Political Context of Education after Devolution*, Policy and Practice in Education 8, Edinburgh: Dunedin Academic Press

PIRLS (2001) *Progress in International Reading Literacy Study*. Available from URL: timss.bc.edu/pirls2001.html (accessed 22 June 2005)

PISA (2004) Newsletter, July 2004. Available from URL: www.oecd.org/dataoecd/28/23/33672578.pdf (accessed 22 June 2005)

Popham, W. J. (1973) *Of Measurement and Mistakes*, Testimony before General Sub-committee on Education, Committee on Education and Labor, House of Representatives, Eric No. ED078020

Powell, J. (1986) *Research Relevant to the 10–14 Report*, Edinburgh: Scottish Education Department

Prenzel, M. and Duit, R. (2000) 'Increasing efficiency of science and mathematics instruction: report of a national quality development programme', paper presented at NARST, New Orleans, April 2000. Available from URL: www.ipn.uni-kiel.de/projekte/blk_sinus.pdf (accessed 22 June 2005)

Press and Journal (1994) 'Parents' voices still loud and clear', 23 August

Primary Education Development Programme (PEDP) (1986) *Practical Guide: Assessment*, PEDP Project, Edinburgh: SED

Raffe, D. (2003) 'CES findings on participation and attainment in Scottish education', in Bryce and Humes (eds) (2003), pp. 795–803

Raffe, D., Howieson, C. and Tinklin, T. (2002) 'The Scottish educational crisis of 2000: an analysis of the policy process of unification', *Journal of Educational Policy*, Vol. 17, No. 2, pp. 167–85

Raffe, D., Howieson, C. and Tinklin, T. (2005) 'The introduction of a unified system of post-compulsory education in Scotland', *Scottish Educational Review*, Vol. 37, No. 1, pp. 46–91

Rowe, M. B. (1974) 'Wait-time and rewards as instructional variables, their influence on language, logic and fate control', *Journal of Research in Science Teaching*, Vol. 11, pp. 81–94

Sadler, R. (1989) 'Formative assessment and the design of instructional systems', *Instructional Science*, Vol. 18, pp. 119–44

Sainsbury, M. and Sizmur, S. (1998) 'Level descriptors in the National Curriculum: what kind of criterion referencing is this?' *Oxford Review of Education*, Vol. 24, No. 2, pp. 181–93

Scotsman (1994a) 'Teachers to boycott tests again', 10 June

Scotsman (1994b) 'Questions on school testing and assessments', (Letters) 29 July

Scottish Council for Research in Education (SCRE) (1977) *Pupils in Profile: Making the Most of Teachers' Knowledge of Pupils*, Edinburgh: Hodder & Stoughton

Scottish Education Department (1977a) *The Structure of the Curriculum in the Third and Fourth Years of the Secondary School* (Munn Report), Edinburgh: HMSO

Scottish Education Department (1977b) *Assessment for All: Report of the Committee to Review Assessment in the Third and Fourth Years of Secondary Education in Scotland* (Dunning Report), Edinburgh: HMSO

Scottish Education Department (1980) *Learning and Teaching in Primary 4 and Primary 7*, Edinburgh: SED

Scottish Education Department (1983) *16–18s in Scotland: An Action Plan*, Edinburgh: SED

Scottish Education Department (1987) *Curriculum and Assessment in Scotland: A Policy for the 1990s*, Edinburgh: SED

Scottish Education Journal (2004) 'CPD: a Chartered Teacher candidate writes', *Scottish Education Journal*, Vol. 88, No. 2, Edinburgh: Educational Institute of Scotland, p. 14

Scottish Executive (1999) *HM Inspectors of Schools Review of Assessment in Pre-school and 5–14*. Available from URL: www.scotland.gov.uk/3-14assessment/ (accessed 26 June 2005)

Scottish Executive (2001a) *A Teaching Profession for the 21st Century: Agreement Reached following Recommendations Made in the*

McCrone Report, Edinburgh: Scottish Executive

Scottish Executive (2001b) *Review of Initial Implementation of New National Qualifications*, Edinburgh: Scottish Executive. Available from URL: www.scottishexecutive.gov.uk/library5/government/sepl-06.asp (accessed 29 June 2005)

Scottish Executive (2001c). *Effective Assessment for Scotland's Schools.* Debate in the Scottish Parliament Sept. 2001. Available from URL: www.ltscotland.org.uk/assess/about/history/announce.asp#0 (Accessed 22 September 2005)

Scottish Executive (2002a) *Raising Standards – Setting Targets*, Edinburgh: Scottish Executive. Available from URL: www.scotland. gov.uk/library5/education/targets2001.pdf (accessed 29 June 2005)

Scottish Executive (2002b) *The Standard for Chartered Teachers*, Edinburgh: Scottish Executive. Available from URL: www.scotland. gov.uk/library5/education/sfct.pdf (accessed 25 June 2005)

Scottish Executive (2004a) *A Curriculum for Excellence*, Edinburgh: Scottish Executive

Scottish Executive (2004b) *Assessment, Testing and Reporting 3–14: Our Response*, Edinburgh: Scottish Executive. Available from URL: www.scotland.gov.uk/library5/education/atror-00.asp (accessed 25 June 2005)

Scottish Executive (2004c) *Ambitious, Excellent Schools: Our Agenda for Action*, Edinburgh: Scottish Executive

Scottish Executive (2004d) *A Curriculum for Excellence: Ministerial Response*, Edinburgh: Scottish Executive. Available from URL: www.scotland.gov.uk/library5/education/cermr.pdf (accessed 27 June 2005)

Scottish Executive (2004e) *5–14 Attainment in Publicly Funded Schools*, Edinburgh: Scottish Executive. Available from URL: www.scotland. gov.uk/stats/bulletins/00379-00.asp (accessed 29 June 2005)

Scottish Executive Education Department (2003) *Report of the Sixth AAP Survey of English* (2001). Available from URL: www.scotland. gov.uk/library5/education/aapel-00.asp (accessed 22 June 2005)

Scottish Executive Education Department (2005a) *Education Department Circular No. 02 June 2005: Assessment and Reporting 3–14.* Available from URL: www.scotland.gov.uk/Publications/Search/Q/Subject/464 (accessed 29 June 2005)

Scottish Executive Education Department (2005b) *Report of the Sixth AAP Survey of Science* (2003) (online). Available from URL: www.scotland.gov.uk/library5/education/aapsss03-10.asp (accessed 22 June 2005)

Scottish Labour Party and Scottish Liberal Democrats (2003) *A Partnership for a Better Scotland: Partnership Agreement*, Available from URL: www.scotland.gov.uk/library5/government/pfbs.pdf (accessed 26 June 2005)

Scottish Office (1994) *Higher Still: Opportunity for All*, Edinburgh: The Stationery Office

Scottish Office Education Department (1991) *Guidelines on Assessment 5–14*, Edinburgh: SOED

Scottish Office Education Department (1992) *Upper Secondary Education in Scotland: Report of the Committee to Review Curriculum and Examinations in the Fifth and Sixth Years of Secondary Education in Scotland* (Howie Report), Edinburgh: HMSO

Scottish Office Education and Industry Department (1996) *Achievements of S1 and S2 Pupils in Mathematics and Science*, Edinburgh: SOEID

Sebba, J. and Maxwell, G. (2004) *Case Study: Queensland, Australia. What Works in Innovation in Education*, OECD. Available from URL: www.oecd.org/dataoecd/53/3/34260428.pdf (accessed 30 June 2005)

Senge, P. and Sharmer, O. (2001) 'Community action research', in Reason, P. and Bradbury, H. (eds) *Handbook of Action Research*, London: Sage Publications

Shepard, L. A. (2000) 'The role of assessment in a learning culture', *Educational Researcher*, Vol. 29, No. 7, pp. 4–14

Simpson, M. (1986) 'School-based and centrally-directed curriculum development – the uneasy middle ground', *Scottish Educational Review*, Vol. 18, No. 2, pp. 76–85

Simpson, M. (1997) 'Developing differentiation practices: meeting the needs of teachers and pupils', *The Curriculum Journal*, Vol. 8, No. 1, pp. 85–104

Simpson, M. (2000) *Learning in Classrooms: Past Imperfect, Future Inconceivable?* Inaugural lecture, University of Edinburgh. Available from URL: www.education.ed.ac.uk/es/ms/index.html (accessed 25 June 2005)

Simpson, M. (2001) 'Assessment and differentiation', in D. Scott (ed.) *Curriculum and Assessment: International Perspectives on Curriculum Studies*, Westport, Connecticut: Ablex, pp. 25–40

Simpson, M. and Arnold, B. (1984) *Diagnosis in Action*, Aberdeen: Aberdeen College of Education

Simpson, M. and Goulder, J. (1998a) 'Promoting continuity and progression: implementing the 5–14 Development Programme in secondary school mathematics and English departments', *Scottish Educational Review*, Vol. 30, No. 1, pp. 15–27

Simpson, M. and Hayward, L. (1998b) 'Policy, research and classroom based development: changing the assessment culture in Scottish schools', *European Journal of Education*, Vol. 33, No. 4, pp. 445–58

Simpson, M. and Payne, F. (2004) *Evaluation of Personalised Laptop Provision in Schools*, Insight No. 14. Available from URL: http://www.scotland.gov.uk/library5/education/ins14-00.asp (accessed 22 September 2005)

Simpson M., Payne, F. and Condie, R. (2005) 'Introducing ICT in secondary schools: a context for reflection on management and professional norms', *Educational Management, Administration and Leadership*, Vol. 33, No. 3 pp. 331–54

Sizmur, S. and Sainsbury, M. (1997) 'Criterion referencing and the meaning of National Curriculum assessment', *British Journal of Educational Studies*, Vol. 45, No. 2, pp. 123–40

Spencer, E. (1987) *Assessment as Part of Teaching*, Edinburgh: Scottish Education Department

Spillane, J. P. (1999) 'External reform initiatives and teachers' efforts to reconstruct their practice', *Journal of Curriculum Studies*, Vol. 31, No. 2, pp. 143–75

Standard Grade Review of Assessment Group (SGROAG) (1986) *Assessment in Standard Grade Courses: Proposals for Simplification*, Edinburgh: Scottish Education Department

Stark, R. (1999) 'Monitoring performance in science: the Scottish approach', *Assessment in Education: Principles, Policy and Practice*, Vol. 6, No. 1, pp. 27-42

Stark, R., Bryce, T. and Gray, D. (1997) 'Four surveys and an epitaph: AAP science 1985–1997', *Scottish Educational Review*, Vol. 29, No. 2, pp. 114–20

Stigler, J. W. and Hiebert J. (1999) *The Teaching Gap*, New York: Free Press. Available from URL: www.pims.math.ca/education/2004/workshop/and/stigler04.html (accessed 22 June 2005)

Third International Mathematics and Science Survey (TIMSS) (1998) Repeat Video Project. Available from URL: www.iea.nl/iea/hq/index.php?id=84&type=1 (accessed 22 June 2005)

Thorpe, G. (2004) *PISA: Initial Report on Scotland's Performance in Mathematics, Science and Reading*, Edinburgh: SEED. Available from URL: www.scotland.gov.uk/library5/education/pisa03.pdf (accessed 30 June 2005)

Times Educational Supplement Scotland (1997a) 'In a class of their own', 3 October

Times Educational Supplement Scotland (1997b) 'Left in the dark on improving maths', 19 September

Times Educational Supplement Scotland (2005) 'University rocket for maths and science', 9 September

Toner, B. (2004) 'Hit by a hangover over in assessment', *Times Educational Supplement Scotland*, 2 January

Torrance, H. and Prior, J. (2001) 'Developing formative assessment in the classroom: using action research to explore and modify theory', *British Educational Research* Journal Vol. 27, No. 5, pp. 615–31

Trends in International Mathematics and Science Study (TIMSS) (2004) International Science Report of 2003 Survey. Available from URL: timss.bc.edu/timss2003.html (accessed 22 June 2005)

Trends In Mathematics and Science Achievement (TIMSS) (1999).

Trends in Mathematics and Science Achievements Around the World. Available from URL: timss.bc.edu/timss1999.html (accessed 22 June 2005)

Tuck, R. (1999) 'The Scottish Qualifications Authority', in Bryce and Humes (eds) (2003), pp. 699–712

Weiss C. H. (1995) 'The four 'I's' of school reform: how interests, ideology, information, and institution affect teachers and principals', *Harvard Educational Review*, Vol. 65, No. 4, pp. 571–93

Wells, M. (1997) 'Scots pupils lag behind in maths and science', *Scotsman*, 26 September

Whetton C. (1997) 'The psychometric enterprise', in S. Hegarty (ed.) *The Role of Research in Mature Educational Systems*, Slough: National Foundation for Educational Research, pp. 97–126

Whetton, C., Twist, E. and Sainsbury, M. (2000) 'National tests and target setting: maintaining consistent standards', paper presented at the American Educational Research Association Annual Conference, New Orleans, 25 April 2000. Available from URL: 195.194.2.34/research/conference list.asp (accessed 23 June 2005)

Wilson J. (2003) 'Mathematics education', in Bryce and Humes (eds) (2003), pp. 558–63

Woessmann, L. and West, M.R. (2002) 'Class size effects in school systems around the world: evidence from between-grade variation in TIMSS' (online). Available from URL: ideas.repec.org/p/kie/kieliw/1099.html (accessed 22 June 2005)

Worthington A. (MP) (1990) 'Why Labour will axe the tests', *Times Educational Supplement Scotland*, 30 November

INDEX